KATE HAXELL

The stitch BIBLE

A comprehensive guide to 225 embroidery stitches and techniques

PROJECT EMBROIDERY BY BECKY HOGG

D&C
David and Charles
www.rucraft.co.uk

CONTENTS

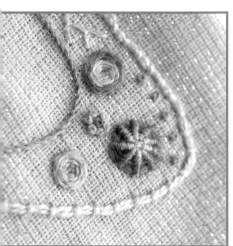

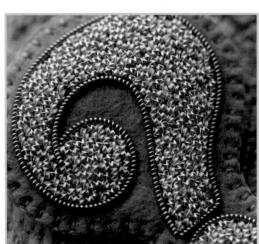

Introduction

Like most little girls in the 1970s I did sewing at school as part of what was then called 'Domestic Science'. We learnt basic dressmaking, simple embroidery, cooking (mainly cakes, as I recall) and how to lay a table properly for different courses. All of these things have stood me in good stead since, and some of them have gone on to become both happy pastimes and a means of earning a living. I started embroidery by stitching a binka dressing table-mat for my grandma, then an owl cushion cover (also on binka), and finally a stitch sampler about which I remember little other than that it featured a house and – spectacularly unoriginally – fern stitch to describe plants.

I carried on embroidering in a rather haphazard way for many years, and then I discovered the Royal School of Needlework at Hampton Court Palace. The RSN was a revelation: I find it so inspiring to spend time in an environment where learning how to work a stitch beautifully is taken completely seriously. And learning those stitches in a building as fabulous as the Palace is quite simply a treat for the eyes and imagination. As with any discipline, there are some aspects of embroidery that I have loved and others that have not been so enchanting; discovering both is part of the pleasure, as one can happily decide never to attempt certain techniques again.

As I learned and improved I was surprised to find how few contemporary embroidery reference books there are. There were quite a lot of technical books published in the 1970s (some of which feature projects I can only describe as remarkable), and many craft sewing books published since, but little in the way of modern, serious instruction books, and nothing that combined solid stitch references for multiple techniques with contemporary projects I actually wanted to make. Fortunately I was not the only person who thought this, and so this book came to be. It provides a winning combination of accurate, clear instruction diagrams for a huge number of stitches across a wide range of techniques, plus creative and easy-to-make projects in which you can exploit the stitches you have mastered.

I have brilliant tutors at the RSN, so when I was asked to put this book together I was able to call upon the best possible professional stitching. I put together a project list, consulted with Becky, she embroidered, and I turned the embroideries into the featured projects. Each of the embroidery techniques featured offers two projects; one simple piece to get you started, and a second design using a wider range of stitches for you to try out. Projects have templates or charts as appropriate, and you'll find those on pages 170–173. The emphasis is on the embroidery, so all the projects are simple to make up, involving only basic sewing skills. However, if sewing is not your thing, you can simply work an embroidery and have it framed as a picture: it will be lovely.

At the beginning of the book are step-by-step instructions for the basic embroidery essentials (preparing fabric, choosing threads, using a frame; those kinds of things), plus some professional techniques that'll help your work look brilliant. If you have never embroidered anything at all before, read through this Getting Started section, then turn to page 24 where you'll find a truly simple yet good-looking drawstring bag that needs only two very easy stitches to make the pretty snowflake pattern that decorates it. From there you can plunder the pages at will: as well as freestyle embroidery, blackwork, crewelwork, goldwork and canvaswork, the three most common whitework techniques – Hardanger, pulled thread and drawn thread – are also included for you to try. (Whitework is so called because traditionally these techniques are worked with white threads on white fabrics.) If you're a novice at a particular technique then you'll find all the information you need to get started, and if you're already a keen embroiderer then there are myriad stitches to occupy your needle.

I encourage you to look upon the projects as a starting point for your embroidery explorations: pick your favourite thread colours instead of Becky and my choices, substitute stitches you love for those favoured here, or use your own original motifs in place of those supplied. Embroidery is not only a therapeutic and absorbing way to spend time, it is also an excellent way to express yourself creatively, so please do indulge yourself in the wealth of stitching on offer in *The Stitch Bible*.

Kate Haxell

GETTING STARTED

Very little is required for your first adventures in embroidery; some fabric, threads, a needle, a simple frame, scissors and a fabric marker will see you through a few projects. However, there are other items that will become essential if you want to do more – and better – embroidery, and some items that are useful, but not vital. The following pages illustrate equipment and explain the techniques needed to make the most of it. In this chapter you will also find the most basic embroidery stitches and a very simple Snowflake Drawstring Bag (see page 24) as a first project.

Equipment

Basic embroidery equipment is both inexpensive and widely available in craft shops and on-line, so you will have no problems finding what you need. It is worth buying good-quality needles and thread, and the best embroidery scissors that you can afford.

FABRICS

Different styles of embroidery require different fabrics and you will find advice on special fabrics at the start of chapters where appropriate. Added to that there is personal taste and any practical considerations.

Plain-weave fabric in linen or cotton is the classic embroiderer's fabric and an excellent choice for beginners to freestyle embroidery (see page 26). These fabrics handle well and have a smooth, tightly woven finish that is easy to work with. If the finished item is likely to be laundered then wash the fabric before you begin stitching to pre-shrink it.

Evenweave fabric has the same number of warp and weft strands to the inch and is designed for counted thread work, such as cross stitch (see page 23), Hardanger (see page 46), blackwork (see page 66), pulled thread (see page 118), and drawn thread (see page 156). You can buy evenweave in 100 per cent linen and cotton, and in some synthetic and natural fibre mixes. Evenweave fabric is graded by the number of strands to the inch (also called 'threads per inch'), that is, the number of warp or weft strands of fabric in a measured inch. This ranges between 12 and 32, with 32 being the finest. A fabric with 24 or 26 strands per inch is suitable for a beginner to try most counted thread techniques.

Aida is a type of evenweave fabric made from 100 per cent cotton and is woven in clearly defined blocks to make stitching very easy. The sizes of these blocks determine the size of the stitches. Aida is generally available in counts of 7, 10, 11, 12, 14, 16, 18 and 22 blocks per inch. You will usually be working each stitch over one block, so if you use 11-count Aida you will fit 11 stitches on one inch of the fabric. If you are a counted thread embroidery novice, Aida is great for your first few projects.

Hardanger is a specialist evenweave fabric for stitching the embroidery style of the same name (see page 46). It usually has 22 strands to the inch and is woven with pairs of strands separated with distinct holes for the stitches, making it very easy to count the strands. Hardanger fabric is also stiffer than many other evenweave fabrics so that it can support the stitching effectively.

Crewel linen twill is a medium-weight twill made specifically for hand embroidery; it's sometimes called 'Jacobean twill'. It is a very finely, tightly woven fabric and the weave does not split, separate or loosen as you pierce the fabric with the needle. Do not use an upholstery twill as a substitute because it will not be tightly woven enough. As the name suggests, crewel twill is the best fabric for crewelwork embroidery (see page 84), and you can also work freestyle embroidery (see page 26) on it. A good-quality herringbone weave fabric or a plain weave can be used instead of twill.

Silk can give embroidery a lavish, elegant look. You can work on fine silks, but for most purposes a firm silk – such as washed silk, thick habutai, dupion, raw silk or taffeta – is best. Silk is often used for goldwork (see page 106), but can be used for freestyle embroidery (see page 26) as well. Silk fabric should usually be stabilised onto calico (see page 14) before being embroidered.

Woven canvas is the fabric used for canvaswork (see page 138). This is a wide-weave fabric with very distinct holes to accommodate thicker threads and wools, and it comes in two forms. Single canvas is woven with just one warp and weft strand between each hole. Like evenweave fabric (see opposite) it is graded by strands to the inch, and can have from 10 to 24 strands. This canvas is suitable for most kinds of canvas stitches. Double canvas (sometimes called Penelope canvas) has two strands between each hole and is used for tramming or for very fine stitching.

THREADS

There is a huge range of threads available and many pages would be required to discuss them all. Therefore, shown and explained here are just the threads used in this book.

Anchor Coton à Broder is a tightly twisted, 3-ply mercerised 100 per cent cotton with a lustrous finish. It is most commonly used for blackwork (see page 66) and whitework (see pages 46, 118 and 156), but it can be used for any surface embroidery. It is available in six tickets, or weights, with ticket 16 being the most popular. This ticket is available in a good range of colours, while the others are only available in black, white and off-white.

Anchor Pearl Cotton is a 2-ply, loosely cabled thread made from 100 per cent Egyptian cotton, and it has a silky finish. It is available in several thicknesses – 3, 5, 8 and 12, with 12 being the finest – and in a wide range of colours. This thread is commonly used for counted thread techniques, but can be used in almost any style of embroidery.

Anchor Stranded Cotton is a very versatile embroidery thread and is used in many techniques. It is made of 100 per cent cotton and is composed of six separate very fine strands. Stranded cottons are the most popular embroidery thread because the fine strands can be split off into smaller groups – usually two or three strands – to create delicate stitching. There is a huge range of colours in the Anchor collection of stranded cottons.

Anchor Tapisserie Wool is 4-ply woollen thread made from 100 per cent pure new wool and is used for canvaswork (see page 138). The tight twist of the plies helps minimise fraying and fluffing as the thread is drawn through the canvas. The thread is also mothproof, which is important when it comes to wool! Again, the Anchor collection has a huge range of colours to choose from.

Appletons Crewel Wool is loosely twisted 2-ply wool thread made from 100 per cent, mothproofed wool. It is a fine wool with a soft, matte finish and comes in a wide range of colours. The loose twist means that it will fluff if the lengths used are too long – 30cm (12in) is a good length to use – and it can become untwisted as you stitch.

Metal threads are used specifically for goldwork (see page 106), and you will find more detailed information on them in that chapter. The samples shown here are gold and silver Japanese (or Jap) thread, gold and copper pearl purl and smooth purl, gold bright check, silver and gold twist, and gold plate.

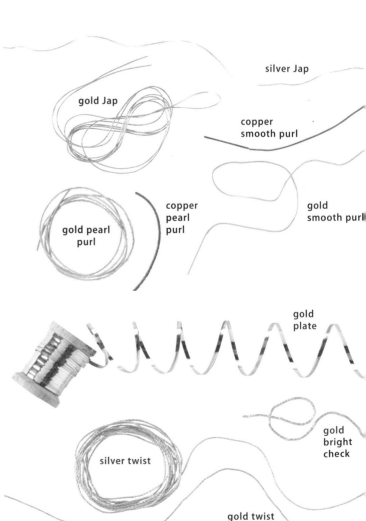

silver Jap

gold Jap

copper smooth purl

gold pearl purl

copper pearl purl

gold smooth purl

gold plate

silver twist

gold bright check

gold twist

NEEDLES

There are many types of needles for the many types of sewing that exist, and here are just the needles you will need to tackle the techniques in this book. Needles are graded in size by number, with the largest number denoting the finest, and shortest, needle of any type. The needle you use needs to have an eye large enough to easily accommodate the thread you want to use, but not so large that it distorts the weave of the fabric as you push it through: the needle should not make a hole larger than the thread is thick.

Embroidery needles have a sharp point and elongated eye, which makes it easier to thread them. They are sometimes called 'crewel needles'. Embroidery needles come in sizes 1–12 and as a guide, use a size 6 or 7 needle with three strands of Anchor Stranded Cotton and a size 5 needle with all six strands. Use a size 5 or 6 needle with Anchor Pearl Cotton no. 5.

Chenille needles are like embroidery needles but with thicker stems and they come in sizes 13–26. Use them when working with heavier threads or on coarse fabrics.

Tapestry needles have a blunt point and large eye and come in sizes 12–28. They are mainly used for canvaswork (see page 138) and some of the counted thread techniques, but are also useful if you need to weave in a thread without piercing the fabric; for example, you will need one for ribbed wheel filling stitch (see page 60).

Bracing needles are very large, sharp needles used for fastening the sides of fabric into a roller or slate frame (see below). You can use a large chenille needle instead, though you may have to use a finer string than is ideal.

Curved needles are useful for lacing up the back of a piece of embroidery (see page 21) before framing it, although not essential.

keep it sharp

Remember that needles do become blunt. Once a needle starts to catch in the fabric, or if it does not pierce the fabric cleanly, change it.

FRAMES

It is always best to work on embroidery in a frame of some sort. The frame will keep the fabric taut as you stitch, preventing the finished piece looking puckered and distorted, and most people find it easier to use a frame than to work on loose fabric. The type of frame depends on the size and style of the embroidery being worked. A ring frame is shown here, and on pages 18–19 you'll find instructions for fixing fabric into all three types of frame.

Ring frames are the most commonly used type and are perfect for fairly small embroideries on fabric. They come in a range of sizes from 10cm (4in) across upwards. You can buy a couple of useful accessories for a ring frame; a table clamp and a seat stand. The table clamp will fix to the edge of a table and the frame fits onto it, so you have both hands free to stitch. A seat stand is a flat wooden base that the frame fits onto and that you then sit on. This allows you to sit in comfort on your sofa with both hands free for stitching.

Roller frames are used for larger pieces of embroidery and for canvaswork. They are widely available and you can buy large floor stands for them that let you sit up to the frame and stitch with both hands.

Slate frames are the type of frame used by professional embroiderers for all large fabric and canvas pieces. They hold the fabric perfectly flat and taut while you work, though it does take a while to fix the fabric into the frame. The large frame should be supported on trestles or a stand for the perfect stitching position.

SCISSORS

You will need two pairs of scissors for most embroideries; a pair of fabric shears for cutting background fabric to size and a pair of embroidery scissors for cutting threads. Buy the best you can afford. Paper scissors for cutting out templates will be useful.

Fabric scissors can have straight or bent blades, and must never ever be used for cutting paper; it really does dull the blades.

Embroidery scissors should have long slim blades with sharp points. You can buy bent embroidery scissors, as shown, which make cutting into corners easier. If you are doing goldwork you should keep a pair of embroidery scissors just for cutting metal threads, as these will blunt the blades.

FABRIC MARKERS

Usually an embroidery design will be a template or sketch that needs to be transferred onto the fabric (see page 15) using a marker. There are various styles of marker you can use, depending on the type of embroidery you are doing. Always, always test a marker on a scrap of the project fabric before drawing up the design. Check that the mark is clearly visible and that it doesn't smudge or spread on the fabric.

Fading fabric markers come as two types; ones that fade in the air and ones that fade when wetted. Water-soluble markers will fade from moisture in the air over time. Therefore, while both types are easy to use, they are not a good idea if you are going to set embroideries aside for weeks at a time.

Chalk pencils are traditional tailor's tools. You can now buy mechanical chalk pencils, as shown, which draw very fine lines. Any visible lines can usually be brushed away once the work is done, but do test this on a scrap of the project fabric first as some lines need to be dampened to disappear.

Permanent marker pens can be used for drawing a design onto canvas. The canvas will be completely covered by stitches, so no lines will show on the finished piece. A fine-tipped felt marker in black is best.

Prick and pounce is the traditional method of transferring a design onto fabric, and it is as efficient today as it was a century ago. This professional method allows very fine detail to be transferred and the final lines do not fade or smudge on the fabric.

OTHER EQUIPMENT

The following pieces will be useful as you do more embroidery, or are needed for specific types of embroidery. Some of these are things you will already have at home if you do any sewing, otherwise you should buy them only as you need them.

An iron will be needed to press any creases out of the embroidery fabric before you start stitching. Check the fabric fibre content and set the iron to a suitable heat.

Pins are useful when finishing the work, or for holding tissue over it to protect it when you are not stitching. Use slim glass-headed ones that won't mark the fabric and are easy to find again.

Thimbles can save the tips of your fingers when stitching, especially when working with metal threads. As well as traditional metal thimbles, you can buy leather and rubber ones; so pick what you prefer. Metal thimbles come in different sizes, so get one that fits or it will be uncomfortable to use. You can also buy rubber needle grabbers, which help you to grip the needle when pulling it through a densely worked area of stitching.

Tweezers are great for picking out ends of thread if you make a mistake and need to unpick. They are also needed for pulling out threads in Hardanger (see page 46) and drawn thread (see page 156) embroidery. You can use eyebrow tweezers, or craft ones that open when you squeeze them and close when you release your grip.

Masking tape can be used to carefully dab up any stray bits of thread fluff after unpicking. Choose a low-tack type so the fabric is in no danger of becoming sticky.

Daylight bulbs are great for embroiderers as they both reduce eye strain and help you to see colours properly. If you are going to be stitching in the evenings, then a positionable lamp with a daylight bulb is a must.

Magnifiers are very useful for fine embroidery, or if your eyesight is not as good as it once was. You can buy magnifiers that are on a headband and can be positioned in front of your eyes, ones that hang around your neck and prop against your chest, and ones that clip onto your embroidery frame. Some of the clip-on variety have lights built into them, which makes them doubly useful.

A tape measure will be needed for measuring the finished embroidery for framing or making up.

Goldwork (see page 106) requires a velvet board, a mellor and beeswax. The velvet board will help stop pieces of metal thread jumping about as you cut them, and can be just a square of thick cardboard with velvet stuck to it. A mellor is a specialist tool for positioning metal threads (although once you have one you'll find it handy for guiding threads in all types of embroidery). Beeswax is used for strengthening thread for some goldwork techniques.

Designing your own embroideries is something many people find very fulfilling. Try to carry a little notebook and a pencil at all times as you really never do know when you'll come across something inspiring. A quick sketch (only for you, it doesn't have to be brilliant) or a written note will be very helpful later on. If you have a camera with you, or a mobile phone with a camera, a snapshot is ideal, but if it is someone else's work you are photographing, always ask their permission first. To develop your designs later all you'll need is paper, pencil, rubber, ruler and maybe compasses.

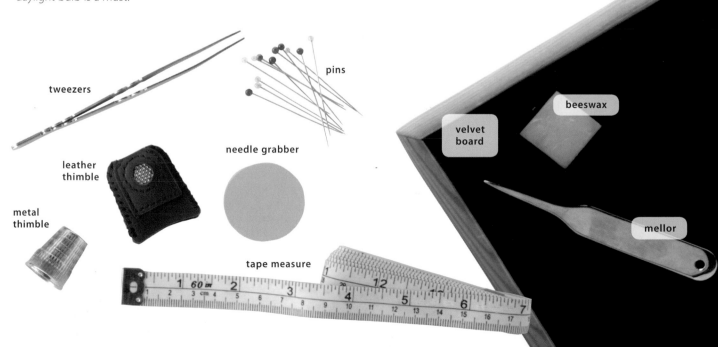

tweezers

pins

leather thimble

needle grabber

metal thimble

tape measure

beeswax

velvet board

mellor

Techniques

There are not many techniques you need to master in order to stitch gorgeous embroideries, and none of them are difficult. If you are new to something, read the instructions through before you start, take your time, and if you need to cut fabric, double-check the measurements before doing so.

PREPARING FABRIC

Specialist embroidery fabrics will usually be ready to stitch as bought; all they'll need is a quick press to remove any creases.

If you are using a fabric not specifically designed for embroidery it is a good idea to wash it to pre-shrink it and test it for colourfastness before starting stitching. If the embroidered item will be washed then it's safest to wash the fabric before starting, even if it's a specialist embroidery fabric.

Fabric that frays a lot, such as silk or velvet, can have the edges neatened by zigzagging them with a sewing machine before framing them. If you are using a roller frame, then you should neaten the edges of plain-weave or evenweave fabrics as well. It's a good idea to stick masking tape over the edges of canvas in a roller frame to stop the embroidery wools catching on the stiff strands.

If you are mounting fabric into a roller or slate frame (see pages 18–19), then the fabric grain needs to be square in the frame. If the grain is obvious, then just cut along it. Otherwise, fray out the edges of the fabric until one strand runs right along the edge and trim off excess threads.

STABILISING FABRIC

Thin fabric, such as silk, velvet or fine linen, that is to be used as a background for freestyle (see page 26), crewelwork (see page 84) or goldwork (see page 106) embroidery will need to be stabilised onto calico before embroidering it. This is best done with the fabric in a roller or slate frame.

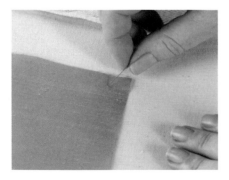

1 Frame up (see pages 18–19) a piece of calico that is larger than the piece of thin background fabric. Pull the calico gently taut, not completely tight. Lay the background fabric centrally on the calico and pin it in place at the corners, making sure it is flat.

2 Using herringbone stitch (see page 39) and sewing thread, sew the fabric to the calico all around the edges.

3 Transfer the design onto the fabric (see pages 15–17). Using a needle and sewing thread to match the fabric, work tiny stab stitches about 2cm (¾in) apart along the design lines to anchor the layers. Pull the calico tight in the frame and you are ready to embroider.

TRANSFERRING A DESIGN

If you are going to embroider some of the projects in this book, or stitch a design from a drawing of your own, you'll need to transfer the motif (see pages 170–171 for project templates) onto the background fabric. There are various ways of doing this, depending on the fabric you are using and the amount of detail in the design.

(see pages 170–171 for project templates)

positioning the design

Some transfer methods are best done on loose fabric and others on framed fabric; advice is given with each method. If you are using loose fabric, you will need enough fabric free around the edges of the design to frame it up (see pages 18–19) and work comfortably on it. The grain of the fabric will also need to be square in the frame, so position the design accordingly.

TRACING OVER A LIGHT SOURCE

Tracing over a light source is quick and easy to do before the fabric is framed up. Ideally use an air-soluble embroidery marker, which will fade over time, though a water-soluble one is fine, too (see page 12). You need to be working on a fairly thin, pale-coloured fabric to use this technique.

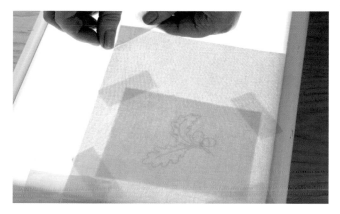

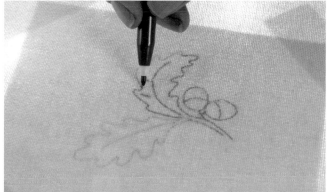

1 Print the motif out onto thin paper or trace it onto tracing paper with a fine black pen. Using masking tape, tape the tracing onto a light box or (in daylight) a window, then tape the fabric right side up on top. Make sure that the fabric is taut and the design is positioned correctly under it.

2 Carefully draw over the design lines with the fabric marker. Remove the tape and frame up the fabric (see pages 18–19).

DRAWING ONTO CANVAS

This is another quick and easy technique and is used just for canvas. You can do this with the fabric loose or framed up. If the fabric is framed, you will have to raise the design up by placing a box or books under it so that the canvas can sit directly on the paper.

1 Right side up, tape the design to a flat surface with masking tape. Tape the canvas over it. Using a permanent marker pen (see page 12), carefully draw over the lines.

USING DRESSMAKER'S CARBON PAPER

This paper can be used on any smooth fabric before it is framed up, and is a good choice for coloured fabric because you can select a carbon colour that really shows up. If the transferred line is faint in places it can be reinforced with a fading fabric marker (see page 12).

1 Print the design out or trace it onto tracing paper with a fine black pen. Using masking tape, tape the fabric right side up on a flat surface, making sure it is taut, and place the carbon paper coloured-side down on top. Tape the traced design over it, making sure all layers are secure. Draw over the design with a hard pencil or ballpoint pen, pressing firmly.

2 Once you have drawn over all the lines, remove some of the tape and fold back the layers to reveal the fabric, making sure you do not disturb the position of the upper layers. If necessary, replace the upper layers and retrace any faint lines before separating the layers completely.

TACKING

Tacking is an easy method of transferring a fairly simple pattern – with an intricate design it will take a long time to tack over all the lines. This method has the great advantage that it leaves no mark on the fabric. Tacking is best done once the fabric has been framed up.

1 Trace the design onto tissue paper that tears easily. Don't be tempted to use tracing paper or printer paper because it will be so hard to tear off that it may distort or break the tacking stitches. Pin the tracing right side up on the fabric.

2 Using sewing thread that contrasts with the fabric colour, tack the paper to the fabric around the edge to secure it. Starting with a knot on the top of the work, sew running stitch (see page 23) over each design line. Keep the stitches fairly small, especially around curves.

3 When all the design lines have been covered, carefully tear off the paper – pulling out any scraps with tweezers – and begin the embroidery. For a medium to large design you can remove the paper only from the part of the design you wish to work first, leaving the paper in place over the remainder to keep the fabric clean.

PRICK AND POUNCE

This is the traditional method used to transfer a design and is still favoured by professional embroiderers. The design lines cannot be removed if you make a mistake, so you do need to be accurate. This method is used with the fabric framed up.

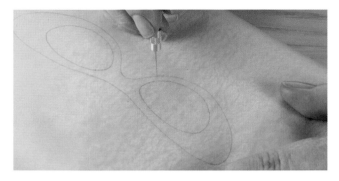

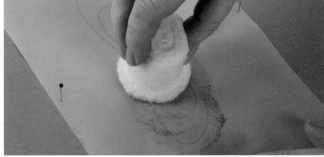

1 Trace the design onto tracing paper with a fine black pen. Lay the tracing on a folded, flat towel and using a medium-sized crewel needle, prick holes along all the design lines. Make the holes close together and ensure that there is a hole at the very start and end of each line and at any corners. You need to hold the needle vertically, and a pricking tool (shown here) clamps the needle firmly and makes it easier to hold, but it isn't essential.

2 Pin the pricked tracing to the fabric, positioning it as required. Choose a pounce powder that will show up on the fabric. Dip the felt dabber into the powder then, starting on one edge, rub powder in a firm circular motion over the tracing, pushing it into the pricked holes. Cover the whole tracing in this way.

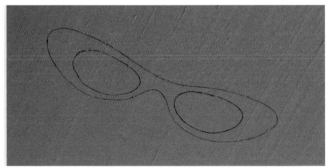

3 Carefully unpin the tracing and lift it directly off the fabric without smudging the dotted powder lines. In a small dish, dilute a little watercolour paint (of a colour that will show on the fabric; white or grey is usually best) with water to a thin consistency. Using a very fine artist's paintbrush, very lightly paint over the design lines. Wipe the brush frequently to stop it clogging with ponce powder. Leave the paint to dry.

4 Standing the frame on edge, firmly tap the back of the fabric with a ruler to knock off any excess powder. You can also use a very soft hairbrush (one made for a baby is ideal) to brush off any remaining powder. The painted lines should be visible but very light, so they can easily be covered by stitching.

ADDITIONAL GUIDELINES

These are extra lines drawn onto the fabric to help work a particular stitch. They can be added when the design is being transferred onto it or just before you work the stitch.

When working, for example, feather stitch (see page 36), your design may only show the outer edges, but it is helpful to mark additional guidelines one-third and two-thirds of the way across the stitch area to ensure that all the stitches are even. Stitches that overlap, such as fishbone stitch (see page 38) and leaf stitch (see page 39), also benefit from additional guidelines to ensure a really smooth result. Make sure you can remove any visible guidelines after completing the stitch.

iron-on transfers

These can be bought commercially with pre-printed designs, or you can buy a special pencil to draw your own transfers. Use them with caution as they require a hot iron (which not all fabrics will react well to) and the lines can spread a bit, making them hard to cover with stitching: lines can't be removed once ironed on.

FRAMING UP FABRIC

It is best to work embroidery with the fabric in a frame rather than holding it loose in your hands. The frame holds the fabric taut while you stitch and the end result will be far more professional looking. There are three main types of frame and here are the methods for fixing fabric into them.

EMBROIDERY HOOP

An embroidery hoop is inexpensive, easy to use and quick to fit or adjust. Hoops come in a variety of sizes and are light to hold. The fabric should be removed after each working session to avoid it marking or stretching around the frame area. Binding the inner ring helps hold the fabric securely and prevent the hoop marking the fabric.

1 Masking tape the bias binding or cotton tape end to the inside of the inner hoop at a 45-degree angle. Wrap it tightly around the hoop, edges overlapping. (If using bias binding, iron one folded side open and overlap the raw edge with the edge still folded.) When you reach the beginning, pin the binding in place and cut off excess. Stitch the end of the binding to the wrapped hoop.

2 Check that the fabric covers the hoop easily then prepare it for framing if need be (see page 14). Lay the bound hoop on a flat surface and lay the fabric right side up on top. If the design is already on the fabric, then make sure it is positioned centrally.

3 Slip the outer hoop down over the top of the inner hoop, sandwiching the fabric between them. If need be, gently and evenly pull on the edges of the fabric to take up any slack within the hoop. Be careful not to pull too much on one side and distort the fabric. Tighten the screw on the hoop, using a screwdriver if necessary.

ROLLER FRAME

Roller frames come in various sizes and are widely available, so they are great for all kinds of embroidery. Modern versions have a handy clipping system that makes them quicker to use, and methods for both modern and traditional types are shown here.

1 For a traditional frame, first cut the fabric to fit. It should be no wider than the webbing on the rollers, but at least as long as the side bars. Neaten and strengthen the edges of fabric with machine zigzag or tape the edges of canvas. Measure from side bar to side bar and mark the middle of the webbing on each roller. Mark the middle of the ends of the fabric that will be sewn to the rollers.

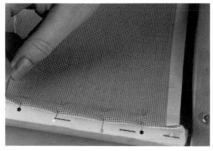

2 Turn under 1cm (⅜in) on the ends of the fabric to be sewn to the webbing and pin one end to the webbing on one roller, matching the marked mid-points. Using strong button thread, oversew the fabric securely to the webbing and remove all pins. Start in the middle and sew out to one edge, then fasten off the thread. Make the stitches irregular lengths to prevent the fabric splitting along one grain line. Return to the middle and sew the other side. Make sure the fabric grain is straight, then sew the other end to the other roller in the same way. Fit the rollers into the side bars and take up the slack in the fabric by turning the rollers outwards and then tightening the nuts.

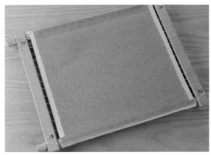

3 To secure the sides of the fabric, use a needle and button thread to lace them over the side bars of the frame. Take a stitch in the fabric, at least 2cm (¾in) in from the edge, then take the thread over and under the adjacent side bar and take another stitch through the fabric.

4 Repeat to the end, then tie the ends of the thread around the corners of the frame. If the fabric is thin then be careful not to damage it by lacing it too tight, though the fabric should be taut in the frame.

5 To fix fabric into a modern version of a roller frame, cut it to fit, then just use the clips to attach the ends of the fabric to the rollers. Turn the rollers to tighten the fabric, then lace the sides as in step 3.

SLATE FRAME

These frames are favoured by professional embroiderers, and while they require the most amount of work to fix the fabric into, the results are certainly worth the effort if you are doing a large or intricate embroidery. The fabric will be held perfectly taut and supported all around.

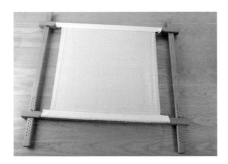

1 Cut the fabric to fit the frame: it should be no wider than the webbing on the top and bottom bars, and no longer than the side bars. Measure and mark the middle of the webbing and fabric as for a roller frame (see opposite), then sew the ends of the fabric to the webbing on the bars in the same way. Insert the side bars into the top and bottom bars and put the metal pegs into holes to hold the fabric taut.

2 Cut a length of woven cotton webbing to fit along each side edge. Pin the webbing to the edge of the fabric, overlapping it by about two-thirds. Sew the webbing in place with horizontal stitches spaced about 2mm (⅛in) and strong button thread, as shown.

3 Lace the webbing strips to the side bars in the same way as for a roller frame, but using string and a bracing needle. Do not pull the string very tight.

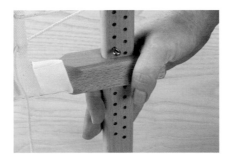

4 To tighten the fabric push the top and bottom bars as far along the side bars as you can, moving the pegs.

5 Finally, tighten the lacing as much as possible and tie the ends of the string around the tops of the side bars.

WORKING FROM A CHART

All counted thread embroidery (see pages 46, 118 and 156) and canvaswork (see page 138) require charts for the individual stitches, and if you are going to follow a design, that will be charted too. There are two main types of chart and both are easy to follow.

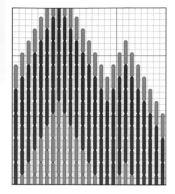

Line charts are the type used in this book. The black grid lines each represent one strand of the evenweave fabric; though if you are stitching on special Hardanger fabric (see page 8), then a line represents a pair of strands. The coloured lines represent the stitches going in and out of the holes in the fabric.

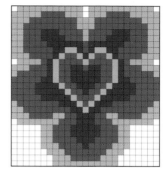

Block charts are usually used for needlepoint designs. Each coloured square represents a stitch worked across one intersection of the canvas.

POSITIONING A CHARTED DESIGN

Counted thread designs usually have charts rather than motifs that need to be transferred, though some have a combination of both. There is an easy way of ensuring that the chart is positioned centrally.

Using a contrast colour sewing thread, tack a line from top to bottom down the exact centre of the fabric. Then tack a horizontal centred line to form a cross. The chart might have arrows at the edges, indicating the middle, but if not it's easy to count the squares and find the middle. Count across the squares on the chart to the edge of the design, then count out from the middle of the tacked cross the same number of strands of fabric; mark the point on the fabric with a pin. Start stitching the design at the marked point and it will be positioned centrally.

THREADING A NEEDLE

This might sound simple, but it's surprising how many people struggle to thread a fine needle, even if they have perfect eyesight. Here are a few tips to make it easier.

Always cut the thread at an angle with sharp embroidery scissors. NEVER bite it through as this just produces a ragged end that's harder to thread.

Don't wet the end of the thread with your lips, that just makes it soggy; if it's a bit fluffy, draw it across some beeswax to smooth and stiffen it.

Hold the thread very close to the end in one hand, and the needle just below the eye in the other hand. Which hand is best for which varies from person to person, so try both ways around to see what suits you.

Make sure the needle is turned so that you can clearly see the whole eye.

Smoothly slide the end of the thread through the eye of the needle.

importance of tension

Successful embroidery requires that you keep the stitches the same length and maintain an even tension. This is really a question of practice. If you are using a new stitch, or working one that you haven't used for some time, work the stitch on a scrap of the project fabric before you begin on the embroidery. Work as many test stitches as it takes to start producing an even line. Time spent doing this will save time unpicking mistakes.

FRAMING AN EMBROIDERY

If you are going to frame a piece of embroidery, it is worth preparing it properly. Having spent the time stitching it, it would be a shame to rush the finishing process.

To centre an embroidery exactly in a frame it helps to have an equal border around the edge of the design. Measure the inside of the frame and add 5–10cm (2–4in) depending on the size of the embroidery. This is the size you want the fabric to be. At the top of the fabric, measure out to each side from the centre of the fabric by half the calculated width and mark this with a pencil. Repeat the process at the bottom and along each side ege, then draw lines between the marks to create a border. Check the measurements by centring the backing part of the frame over the design. You should have a wide border of fabric all around the backing. Check that the design is centred within the drawn frame and that the fabric grain is straight. Trim the fabric along the drawn line.

Now when you lace the embroidery (see below), it should be easy to centre it on the padded board. If desired, you can also draw or tack the fabric where the edges of the board will be to help position it easily and correctly. Although this may seem like extra effort, it makes the next stage much quicker, as well as reducing the possibilities of error.

When you are ready for framing check that the frame and glass are clean and dry on both sides, with no smears on the glass. Lace the embroidery to the board following the instructions below and then fit it neatly in the frame. Seal the back with gummed paper tape, pressing it gently into the rebate. The tape will shrink as it dries, sealing in the picture and helping to keep out dust and tiny insects.

LACING AN EMBROIDERY

Lacing your work stretches it taut and ensures that it will be held neatly in the frame. Use foamcore board, which has a layer of polystyrene sandwiched between layers of thin card, because this enables you to pin the embroidery to the edges. Make sure that you centre the embroidery exactly on the card and use padding to smooth out any lumps.

1 Cut foamcore board and quilt wadding to fit the chosen frame and attach the wadding to the board using glue or double-sided tape. Leave to dry. Lay out your embroidery, face down, and centre the board on top, padded side down.

2 Secure the fabric by pinning into the edges of the foamcore board, working first along one edge and then along the opposite edge. Flip the embroidery over and check that the design is centred. When you are happy with the positioning, flip it back over, fold in the corners diagonally and then pin the remaining sides in place.

3 The edges of a small design can be secured with double-sided tape. For a larger design, lace opposite edges together with strong thread in a large needle, taking a stitch first on one side and then on the other. Pull the thread tight every few stitches. Repeat to lace the remaining opposite sides together. Oversew the mitred corners to finish.

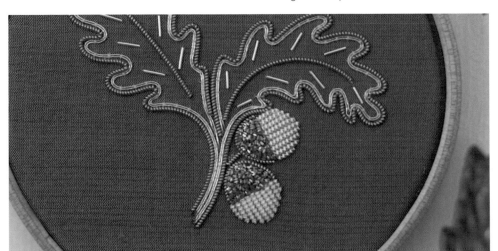

For a contemporary framing idea, turn to page 116.

Starting and finishing stitching

It is best to have the minimum of knots and trailing threads on the back of the work because even when the back will not be on view, knots can cause lumps and trailing threads can show up as shadows on the right side. When stitching use a 30cm (12in) length of thread because longer lengths can knot, separate or fray.

WASTE KNOT METHOD

This method can be used for all styles of embroidery. If the thread is dark, the fabric light in colour and the stitch pattern quite gappy, it may be better to use the in-line method (see below) to prevent the thread showing on the front as a shadow between stitches.

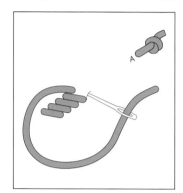

1 Make a good-sized knot in the end of the thread and insert the needle from the right side at A, within the area that will be covered by the stitching. Work the stitches to fill the area, covering and securing the thread on the back of the work at the same time, then cut off the knot. If necessary, work several elements of the design to ensure that the loose thread is secured before cutting off the knot.

IN-LINE METHOD

Use this method when a single row or small area of stitching is being worked and where a waste knot might mark the fabric.

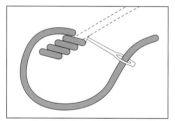

1 Bring the thread out at the start of the row of stitching, leaving a long tail on the back; shown here by the dotted lines. Work the row, making sure that you stitch over and secure the tail of thread on the back. Trim off any excess tail when the row is complete.

STITCHING METHOD

This method can be used when the background fabric is tightly woven and the area will be covered by the stitching.

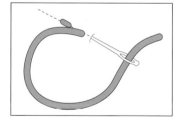

1 Starting on the wrong side, make two very tiny running stitches either on the design line or within an area that will be filled with solid stitching. Each tiny stitch should cover no more than two or three strands of the fabric.

DARNING METHOD

Once one area of a design has been stitched, this method can be used to start thread for stitching adjacent areas.

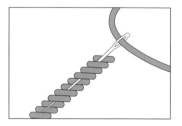

1 On the back of the work, weave the needle in and out of the threads of previous stitches. Take the needle a short distance in one direction, then weave back the other way to secure the thread. Be sure not to pull too hard or weave more than one thread into the back of the same stitches as it might distort the stitching on the front.

FINISHING OFF

Finish off a thread by darning it into the back of the row of stitches in the same way as for darning in a thread to start it (see above).

1 Weave the thread in and out of the back of stitches in one direction then the other, then cut off any excess.

Basic stitches

RUNNING STITCH

Running stitch is the simplest of all embroidery stitches, but it never loses its charm. It is used in the Snowflake Drawstring Bag (see page 24).

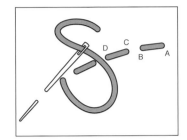

1 Starting at the right-hand end of the design line, bring the needle out at A and insert it at B. Bring it out again at C and insert it at D. Continue in this way, making the stitches of even length and the gaps between them also of even length.

BACKSTITCH

Backstitch is an outlining stitch, producing a solid line that will bend around curves when the stitches are quite short.

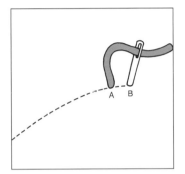

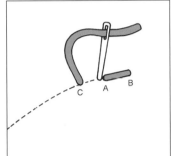

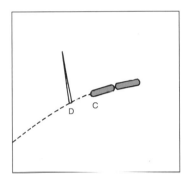

1 Bring the needle out at A, one stitch length from the start of the design line, and insert it at B, at the beginning of the line.

2 Bring the needle out at C, so that A lies halfway between B and C, and re-insert it at A in the hole previously made.

3 Bring the needle out at D, making sure you maintain the same stitch length as before. Insert it at C and continue in this way.

CROSS STITCH

Cross stitch is maybe the most popular embroidery stitch in the world. Easy to work on evenweave fabric (see page 8), it is used in the Snowflake Drawstring Bag (see page 24).

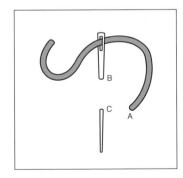

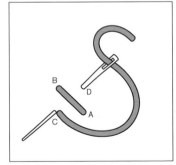

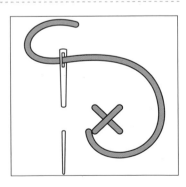

1 Bring the needle out at A on the right-hand side of the design area and make a diagonal stitch to B, an equal distance up and to the left of A. Bring the needle out at C, immediately below B and level with A.

2 Make the second diagonal stitch to D, immediately above A and level with B. To work a second adjoining cross, bring the needle out at C again.

3 Work cross stitches in the same way across the row.

Snowflake drawstring bag

This sweet and very simple-to-make bag can be almost any size; small enough to hold sunglasses (and featuring just one snowflake), or large enough to hold shoes. The Scandinavian-style snowflake motif is easy to work and will stitch up quickly, so even if this is your first ever embroidery project, it won't take long to sew. The version shown here is small shoe-bag size and would be a lovely gift for a child starting dance lessons, or pretty gift wrap – and then useful storage – for new party shoes.

MATERIALS

- Piece of 32-count evenweave fabric in ivory measuring 55 x 40cm (22 x 16in)
- Tape measure
- Tacking thread
- Hand-sewing needle
- Large ring frame
- Snowflake chart (see page 172)
- Anchor Stranded Cotton: one skein of colour 13
- Size 26 tapestry needle
- Scissors
- Piece of medium-weight cotton fabric measuring 45 x 30cm (18 x 12in)
- Pins
- Sewing thread to match fabric
- Sewing machine
- Iron
- Safety pin
- Piece of 1-cm (½-in) wide cotton tape measuring 70cm (27½in) long

STITCHES USED

- Cross stitch (see page 23)
- Running stitch (see page 23)

THE EMBROIDERY

Tack a 45 x 30cm (18 x 12in) rectangle on the fabric, positioning it centrally; this is the size of the bag. Tack a vertical line down the centre of the fabric (see page 20). The band of embroidery can be positioned anywhere on the bag; here is it 5cm (2in) up from the bottom edge of the fabric. Fix the area to be embroidered into a large ring frame (see page 18).

The embroidery is worked in two strands of Stranded Cotton throughout. The first row consists of alternate running stitches over three strands of fabric and cross stitches over two-by-two strands; there is a gap of a single strand between each stitch and the running stitches are centred on the cross stitches. Start the embroidery with a cross stitch on the tacked centre line and work out to one edge, then go back to the centre and work out to the other edge. On each side, stop stitching 1cm (⅜in) in from the edge of the fabric (this will be the seam allowance and threads can be secured within it).

Following the chart, position the first snowflake on the central tacked line, eight strands up from the first row of embroidery. Work the motif in cross stitch only. Work two more snowflakes on either side of the first one, positioning them 27 strands of fabric apart.

Complete the embroidery with another row of running and cross stitches eight strands above the snowflakes.

MAKING UP

Take the fabric out of the frame and cut it down to the tacked rectangle; remove all tacking threads. Pin the embroidery and the cotton fabric right sides together. Set the sewing machine to a small straight stitch and, taking a 1cm (⅜in) seam allowance, sew down one long side, across the bottom and up the other long side. Set the machine to a narrow zigzag stitch and sew around the seam allowances, as close as possible to the stitching. Trim the seam allowances close to the zigzagging. Turn the bag right side out and press it.

On the open top edge, turn under a 1cm (⅜in) then a 2cm (¾in) hem and press, then unfold the hems. On the back fabric, mark a 1.5cm (⅝in) buttonhole on the second fold line, close to one side seam. Sew the buttonhole either by hand using buttonhole stitch (see page 29), or by machine. Refold and pin the hems so that the buttonhole is right on the top edge of the bag. Set the sewing machine to a small straight stitch and sew right around the hems, very close to the lower edge, to make a channel.

Put the safety pin through one end of the tape and use it to thread the tape through the buttonhole, around the channel and out through the buttonhole again. Remove the pin and use your fingers to manipulate the tape in the channel to check it isn't twisted. Overlap the ends of the tape and sew them together, then slip the tape loop around in the channel so that the join is hidden.

getting it right

The nature of the embroidery means that there should be no long threads on the back to get caught on the bag's contents. If you are worried that threads might catch, make up the bag in the same way as the Laundry Bag (see page 168), with a lining to protect the stitching.

FREESTYLE

This chapter covers what most of us would generally call 'embroidery': decorative stitches that are worked on woven fabric – as opposed to canvas or counted thread fabric – using embroidery threads. Of course, once you get started you'll explore further and find that there is much more to freestyle embroidery than this, but this chapter is the perfect starting point if you are an embroidery novice.

The two projects in this section explore different stitches, starting with some very simple ones to embellish the Celebration Bunting (see page 34). The Retro Sunglasses Case (see page 42) introduces some more stitches, and both projects offer great opportunities for using other stitches you like the look of.

Turn to pages 14–23 for general instructions for preparing fabric, transferring a design, and stitching.

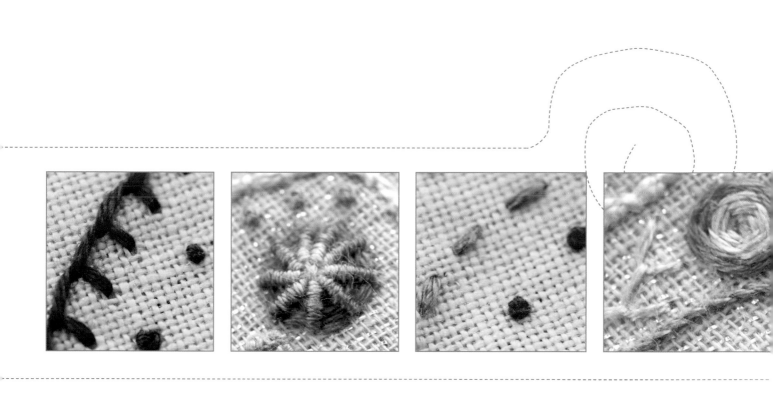

Bokhara Couching

Bokhara couching creates a thick, dense filling, or it can be used as an outline stitch. With most couching techniques one thread is laid across the fabric and then a second, finer thread is used to stitch it down (see page 33). With Bokhara couching the same thread is used for both.

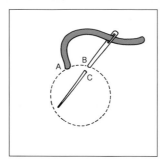

1 Bring the needle out at A, insert it at B and bring it out again at C.

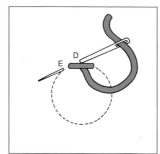

2 Insert the needle at D to trap the laid thread with a slanting stitch, and bring it out at E, ready to lay another thread.

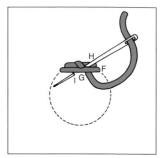

3 Insert the needle at F to lay the thread and bring it out at G, ready to make a slanting stitch. Insert the needle at H and bring it out at I to make the next slanting stitch.

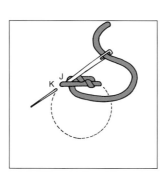

4 Insert the needle at J and bring it out at K, ready to lay another thread. Note how the catching stitches are staggered to enable them to lie neatly and to create an attractive pattern. If desired, the couching stitches can be spaced quite wide apart. Continue in the same way.

Bullion Stitch

Bullion stitch is an individual stitch that can also be grouped to form a motif or filling. Work it in a similar way to a French knot (see page 38), but with more twists around the needle.

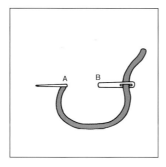

1 Bring the needle out at A, at the start of the stitch. Insert it at the end point, B, and then bring it out again at A. Do not pull the needle right through the fabric.

2 Twist the thread around the needle point five or six times, so that the twists will cover the length between A and B.

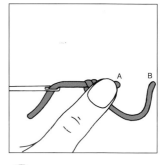

3 Place your thumb on the coiled thread and pull the needle through, taking care not to distort the twists of thread.

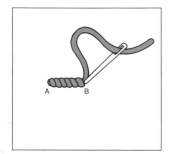

4 Insert the needle at B and gently pull the working thread through until the bullion stitch lies flat.

Buttonhole Stitch

Buttonhole stitch is an edging stitch that can also be worked as an outline, or in a circle to create wheels. The stitches can be butted up closely, or spaced out as in the Celebration Bunting (see page 34). This stitch is also known as blanket stitch.

1 Bring the needle out at A. Insert the needle at B, above and slightly to the right of A, and bring it out at C, directly below B, keeping the working thread under the needle.

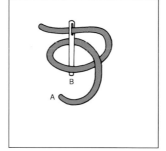

2 Pull the thread through to form the stitch. Insert the needle at D and bring it out at E, directly below D, with the thread under the needle.

3 Continue working stitches as shown, keeping the stitch height and spacing as even as possible.

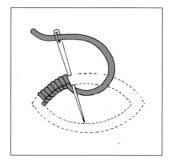

4 When working around curves, fan out the stitches slightly along the top edge to create the shape.

Knotted Buttonhole Stitch

Knotted buttonhole stitch is a decorative version of buttonhole stitch (see above) with a neat knot on the top edge. The stitches can be tightly packed or spaced out.

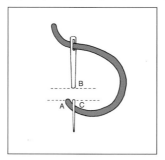

1 Bring the needle out at A, on the lower design line, and make a loop around your finger with the thread. Insert the needle up through the loop.

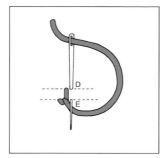

2 Slide your finger out and with the loop still around the needle, insert the needle at B, on the upper design line and slightly to the right of A.

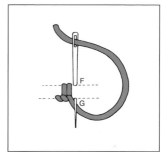

3 Bring the needle out at C, with the thread under the point and, before pulling the needle through, tighten the loop around it by gently pulling the thread.

4 Pull the thread through to form the stitch, then make a loop around your finger for the next stitch.

Cable Stitch

Cable stitch makes a bold, solid outline stitch, but it can also be massed in rows as a filling stitch. Used in this way it is very textural, so be aware that it can look a bit busy in a large area.

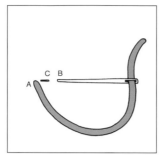

1 Bring the needle out at A, at the start of the stitching line. Keeping the thread below the needle, insert the needle at B, to the right of A, and bring it out at C, midway between A and B.

2 Work the next stitch in the same way, but this time keep the thread above the needle, inserting the needle at D and bringing it out at B.

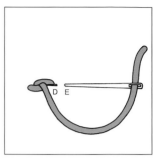

3 Insert the needle at E and bring it out at D, this time with the thread below the needle.

4 Insert the needle at F and bring it out at E with the thread above the needle. Continue in the same way to the end of the line.

Cable Chain Stitch

Cable chain stitch is an outline stitch that looks like chain stitch (see page opposite, above), but with a small link between each chain. Like cable stitch, above, it can also be worked in massed lines as a filling stitch or to create bands.

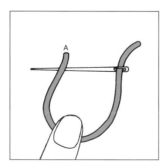

1 Bring the needle out at A and hold the thread down with your finger or thumb. Pass the needle from right to left under the working thread, without piercing the fabric.

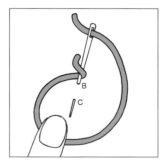

2 Twist the needle back to the right over the working thread and, still holding the thread, insert the needle at B, bringing it out at C. Keeping the thread under the needle, pull the working thread through to form a chain loop.

3 Repeat the process, inserting the needle at D and bringing it out at E to make the next stitch. Continue in this way.

Chain Stitch

Chain stitch can be used as an outline stitch or worked in rows as a lacy filling. It is made by working a series of looped stitches together in a line and it is simple yet satisfying. It is used in the Celebration Bunting (see page 34).

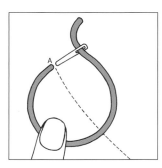

1 Bring the needle out at A, hold the thread down and insert the needle back through the same hole.

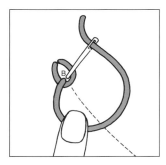

2 Bring the needle out at B and, keeping the thread under the needle, pull it gently to form a loop. Insert the needle back through the hole at B.

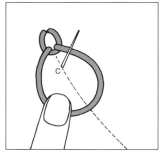

3 Bring the needle out at C to make the next loop in the chain.

even tension

Pull each stitch to the desired size as you work. The stitches are connected, so if you try to make one stitch a little larger later on, you'll find that you are pulling up one of the stitches next to it.

4 Finish the final loop with a small tying stitch, as shown. A single loop held down with a tying stitch is called detached chain stitch.

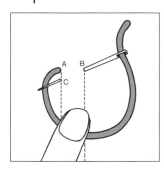

Open Chain Stitch

Open chain stitch, also called square chain or ladder chain stitch, makes a lacy outline or an efficient filling stitch that can be worked to various widths.

1 Bring the needle out at A and insert it to the right at B, level with A. Bring it back out at C, directly below A. Hold the working thread down and under the needle.

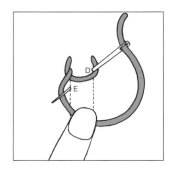

2 Pull the thread through, leaving the loop slightly loose. Insert the needle at D, directly below B and bring it out at E, directly below C. Keep the working thread under the needle, as before.

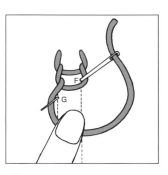

3 Insert the needle at F and bring it out at G. Secure the last loop in the chain with a small tying stitch at each side.

Twisted Chain Stitch

Twisted chain stitch is a decorative outlining stitch, giving textural interest to simple designs. It is ideal for suggesting twining vines or leaf tendrils.

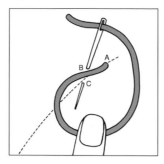 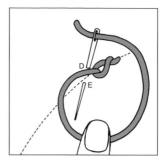 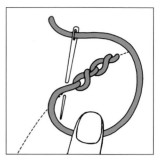

1 Bring the needle out at A and insert it to the side of the design line at B. Take a small, slanting stitch across the line and bring the needle out at C. Pass the thread over and then under the needle, as shown.

2 Gently pull the thread through to form a twisted chain of the desired size. Insert the needle at D and bring it out at E.

3 Pass the thread over and then under the needle and pull it through to form a second stitch. Continue in the same way. Secure the final stitch with a small tying stitch in the same way as for chain stitch (see page 31).

Chained Feather Stitch

Chained feather stitch can be worked as a border stitch or as part of a pictorial design; it's particularly good for describing climbing plants. When working a border, mark both outside edges before you start to avoid stitching off line.

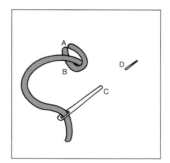 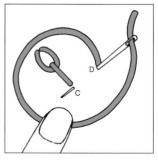 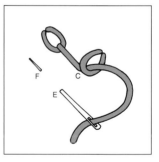

1 Bring the needle out at A and make a slanting chain stitch (see page 31), bringing the needle out at B. Take the needle in at C and bring it out at D, level with B.

2 Holding the thread down as shown, re-insert the needle at D and bring it out again at C.

3 Keeping the thread under the needle, pull it through and insert the needle at E, immediately below B, and bring it out at F, level with C and below A. Continue in this way, making stitches on alternate sides.

Chevron Stitch

Chevron stitch is a zigzag border stitch that can also be worked as a filling. It can be worked open, as shown here, or closed, with the horizontal stitches sharing holes to create the effect of parallel backstitch (see page 23) lines with zigzags in between them.

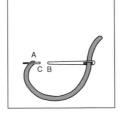 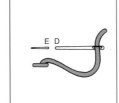  

1 Bring the needle out at A on the lower design line, insert it at B and bring it out at C, halfway between A and B. Keep the working thread below the needle, as shown.

2 Insert the needle at D on the upper design line and take a small stitch to bring it out at E.

3 Insert the needle at F so that D is halfway between E and F. Keep the thread above the needle and bring it out again at D.

4 Insert the needle at G on the lower design line, and bring it out again at H.

5 Insert the needle at I and bring it out at G. Continue in the same way to complete the line of stitching.

Couching

Couching is a means of utilising a thicker, more decorative or more delicate thread than you would be able to stitch with conventionally. This thread is simply laid on top of the fabric and secured with a finer, usually matching, thread. It is used in the Retro Sunglasses Case (see page 42).

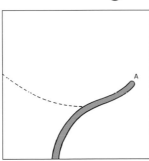 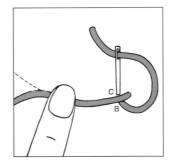 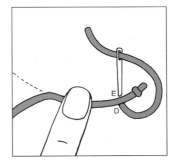

1 Bring the decorative thread through at A and lay it on the design line.

2 Hold the laid thread in position as you work, keeping it fairly taut. Bring the securing thread through at B and insert it at C on the opposite side of the decorative laid thread.

3 Bring the needle out at D, about 5mm (¼in) along the design line from C–B, and insert it at E. Continue until you have secured the entire length of laid thread. Take the free end of the laid thread through to the wrong side and secure both threads.

Celebration bunting

No longer just brought out for parties, festive bunting can now be an interior design accent all year around. It's easy to make from scrap-bag fabrics, and you can make yours extra-special by embroidering the central pennant. This easy-to-work heart motif can be worked in any colour palette; choose one to suit the room you want to hang the bunting in.

MATERIALS

- Piece of cotton fabric measuring 25 x 25cm (10 x 10in)
- Heart template (see page 170)
- Transfer equipment
- 15cm (6in) ring frame
- Anchor Stranded Cotton: one skein in each of colours 11, 29, 42 and 40
- Size 10 embroidery needle
- Paper
- Scissors
- Fading fabric marker
- Pieces of fabric measuring at least 20 x 14cm (8 x 5½in) for pennants
- Pins
- Sewing machine
- Sewing threads to match fabric colours
- Pinking shears
- Knitting needle (optional)
- Iron
- Bias binding 2.5-cm (1-in) wide, measuring long enough to accommodate all the pennants, plus extra for ties at each end
- Sewing thread to match bias binding

STITCHES USED

- Chain stitch (see page 31)
- Buttonhole stitch (see page 29)
- French knots (see page 38)
- Running stitch (see page 23)

THE EMBROIDERY

Using either the tracing over a light source, or dressmaker's carbon technique – depending on the fabric – (see pages 15 or 17), enlarge the design by 200 per cent and transfer onto the large piece of cotton fabric, positioning it centrally. Fix the fabric into the ring frame (see page 18).

Embroider the outer line in buttonhole stitch and three strands of colour 29. Embroider the middle line in running stitch and three strands of colour 40, and the inner line in chain stitch and three strands of colour 11. Use two strands to embroider the French knots (indicated by dots on the template), working the outer row in colour 42 and the inner row in colour 29.

MAKING UP

On paper, draw out the size of the pennant you want. This one is 20cm (8in) across the top and 14cm (5½in) from top to tip. The sloping sides are slightly curved to echo the shape of the heart, but you can just cut a classic triangle; it will look equally good. Cut the pennant shape out of the paper, discarding the cut out and keeping the frame to use as a window template. Take the fabric out of the ring frame. Position the window template over the design to best effect and draw around the edge of the template with the fabric marker.

Cut out the embroidery and a back piece for that pennant, and cut as many other pennants as you want, cutting two pieces for each one. Pin the front and back of each pennant right sides together. Set the sewing machine to a medium straight stitch. Using matching thread, sew the side seams of the pennants, taking 1cm (⅜in) seam allowances and leaving the top edge open.

Trim the seam allowances with pinking shears and turn each pennant right side out, pushing out the point: you may find a knitting needle useful for this, but be careful not to push

it through the fabric. Press the pennants flat.

Fold the bias binding lengthways, folding it so that one side is slightly wider than the other, and press it. The deeper side will be the front. Turn under and press the ends of the binding to neaten them. Mark the mid-point of the binding with a pin. Slip the embroidered pennant into the fold of the binding, positioning it centrally on the pin, then pin it in place. Pin the other pennants into the binding, spacing them equally.

Set the sewing machine to a medium zigzag stitch. Starting at one end, stitch right along the bias binding, close to the open edge, stitching over the pennants and removing the pins as you reach them.

getting it right

If you want to make a lot of bunting, get some friends involved and have a bunting production line party. With one person cutting pennants, someone pinning them, another stitching, one person turning and pressing and someone pinning them into the binding, you can produce a huge amount, and have a fun sewing day.

Cretan Stitch

Cretan stitch is a filling stitch from the feather stitch family. Its open, woven appearance makes it excellent for filling leaf shapes and it can add a lovely, tactile quality to an embroidery.

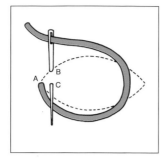

1 Bring the needle out at A and insert it at B. Bring it back out at C, with the thread under the point of the needle.

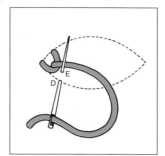

2 Pull the thread through to form a loop and insert the needle at D, bringing it out at E, with the thread under the point.

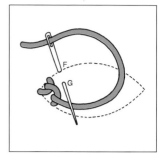

3 Continue in this way, taking the needle down at F and out at G and following the outline of the design.

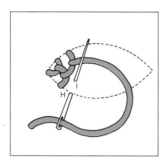

4 Insert the needle at H and out at I, then continue in this way to fill the whole motif.

Feather Stitch

Feather stitch was used to decorate work smocks in the 18th and 19th centuries, together with chain stitch (see page 31) and buttonhole stitch (see page 29), and is still used to decorate hems. It can be used for outlines, or for borders or fillings and is featured in the Retro Sunglasses Case (see page 42).

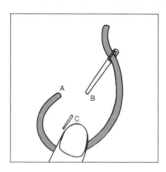

1 Bring the needle out at A and insert it at B on the same level, bringing it back out at C. A, B and C should be equidistant.

2 Insert the needle at D and bring it out at E, keeping the thread underneath. The distances between C, D and E should be the same.

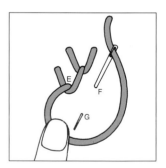

3 Continue working in this way, keeping the thread below the needle. Secure the last loop with a tiny tying stitch.

Spanish Knotted Feather Stitch

Spanish knotted feather stitch is a variation of feather stitch that produces a much denser, ornate look. Use it for thick outlines or very textural fillings.

1 Bring the needle out at A, insert it at B and bring it out again at C. Wrap the thread over and under the needle, as shown.

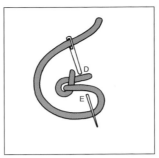

2 Pull the thread through and insert the needle at D, bringing it out at E. Wrap the thread over and under the needle.

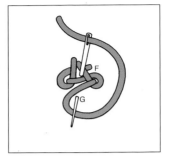

3 Pull the thread through and insert the needle at F, bringing it out at G. Wrap the thread over and under the needle again.

4 Pull the thread through, insert the needle at H and bring it out at I. Wrap the thread over and under the needle. Pull the thread through and continue working Steps 3 and 4.

Fern Stitch

Fern stitch is an easy stitch that creates a feathery effect, ideal for delicate plant designs. It can be worked as an outline or a motif, or massed as a filling.

1 Bring the needle out at A and insert it at B.

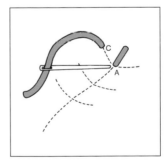

2 Bring the needle out at C then insert it again at A, as shown.

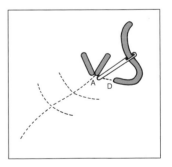

3 Bring the needle out at D and re-insert it at A. This completes a single fern stitch.

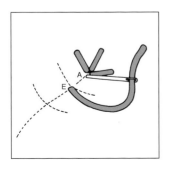

4 Bring the needle out at E and insert it at A. Continue in this way, following the design line.

Fishbone Stitch

Fishbone stitch is a filling that is ideal for leaf shapes. It interweaves at the centre, creating the leaf vein, and the stitches are angled to emphasise the leaf shape.

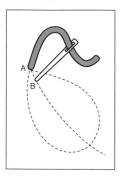 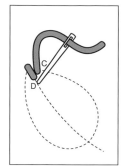 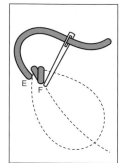 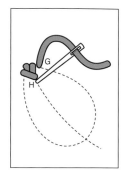

1 Bring the needle out at A and insert it at B, making a small straight stitch along the centre line of the shape.

2 Bring the needle out at C, on the outer edge of the shape and insert it at D next to the base of the first stitch.

3 Bring the needle out at E, on the outer edge of the shape and insert it at F, overlapping the base of the previous stitch.

4 Bring the needle out at G and insert it at H, overlapping the base of the previous stitch. Cover the entire shape in this way, butting the stitches up tightly so there are no gaps.

French Knots

French knots can be worked singly, in rows, or grouped together to create a highly textured filling stitch. These knots are used in both the Celebration Bunting (see page 34) and the Retro Sunglasses Case (see page 42).

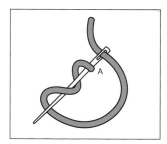  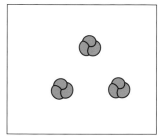

1 Bring the needle out at A, where the knot will be, and wrap the thread once or twice around it.

2 Holding the thread firmly, twist the needle back around and insert it very close to A.

3 Holding the wraps down on the front, pull the thread through and tighten the knot.

working knots

Avoid long threads running across the back of the piece as they may show through as lumps on the front. If you are working a group of French knots, then move from one to the other without cutting the thread. However, if you are working single knots, secure each one with a couple of tiny stitches into the back of it (or the back of adjacent stitching), then cut the thread.

Herringbone Stitch

Herringbone stitch is a very versatile stitch that can be worked as a border, in bands to create textured stripes, or as a filling stitch, although it can look rather busy over a large area.

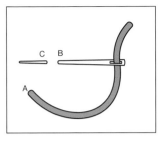

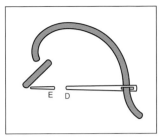

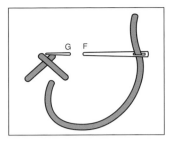

1 Bring the needle out at A on the lower design line. Insert it at B on the upper design line and bring it out at C.

2 Insert the needle at D on the lower design line, bringing it out at E.

3 Insert the needle at F on the upper design line, bringing it out at G.

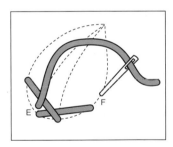

4 Insert the needle on the lower design line at H and bring it out at I. Continue to stitch in the same way.

Leaf Stitch

Leaf stitch is an open filling stitch with a woven central stripe that makes it ideal for describing foliage.

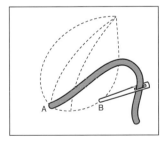

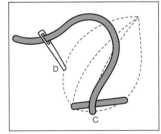

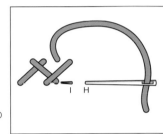

1 Bring the needle out at A and insert it at B to form a sloping stitch.

2 Bring the needle out at C and insert it at D.

3 Bring the needle out at E and insert it at F.

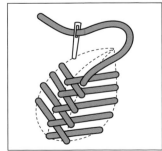

4 Continue the sequence, working evenly-spaced stitches on alternate sides to fill the whole shape.

Rope Stitch

Rope stitch is quick and easy to work and can be used either as an attractive outline, or to describe elements of trees and plants, and, of course, rope.

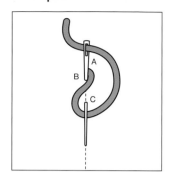 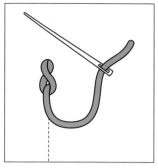 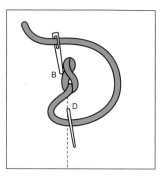

1 Bring the needle out at A, insert it at B and bring it back out at C on the design line, twisting the thread over and under the needle, as shown.

2 Set the stitch by firmly pulling the thread through and downwards to form a twisted loop.

3 Insert the needle again at B, in the curve of the first stitch, and bring it out at D with the thread under the needle, as before. Continue in the same way, keeping the tension even.

Satin Stitch

Satin stitch is a filling stitch consisting entirely of straight stitches. It takes practice to make the surface smooth and the edges even, but when worked well it is invaluable to the embroiderer. Split stitch (see opposite) can be used to outline the shape first if desired; the satin stitches are then worked immediately outside the outline.

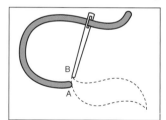 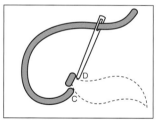

1 Bring the needle out at A and insert it at B, working on the design lines.

2 Bring the needle out at C and insert it at D. Continue working across the shape in this way, placing the stitches very close together so that no background fabric shows. Keep the edges of the shape even and neat.

stitch direction

Satin stitches can be worked in different directions to emphasise areas of a design. For example, when embroidering a bird the stitches can follow the direction the feathers lie in to help describe them more fully.

Scroll Stitch

Scroll stitch is a knotted, wavy outline stitch that adds instant texture to a simple design. Try using it in conjunction with other stitches to create decorative bands.

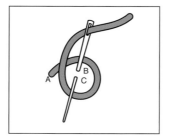

1 Bring the needle out at A and insert it at B, bringing it back out at C. Wrap the thread behind the needle and under the point, as shown, then pull the needle through to form the stitch.

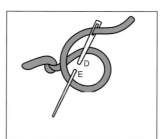

2 Insert the needle at D and bring it out at E, wrapping the thread around it as before. Continue stitching in this way.

Split Stitch

Split stitch is a delicate outline stitch that, when worked correctly, looks like very fine chain stitch. It can also be used to define the edges of a shape before that shape is filled with satin stitch (see opposite).

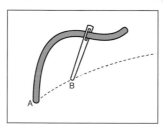

1 Bring the needle out at A and insert it at B.

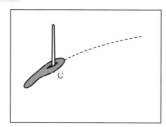

2 Bring the needle out at C, piercing the thread of the previous stitch.

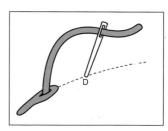

3 Insert the needle at D to form the next stitch. Then bring the needle up to pierce the stitch just worked, as before. Make all the stitches the same length and pierce them at the same point to create an even outline.

Retro sunglasses case

This wonderfully witty pouch to store your sunglasses in is easy to make. The embroidered vintage glasses are studded with 'jewels' created with two types of wheel stitches and French knots. The embroidery will span your knowledge of stitches if you follow the template given, but you can easily adapt the glasses design to include other favourite stitches if you prefer.

MATERIALS

- Piece of outer fabric measuring 25 x 25cm (10 x 10in)
- Sunglasses template (see page 170)
- Transfer equipment
- 20cm (8in) ring frame
- Size 10 embroidery needle
- Anchor Stranded Cotton: one skein in each of colours 185, 186, 187, 188 and 1017
- Anchor Pearl Cotton No. 8: one ball in colour 213
- Paper
- Pencil
- Fading fabric marker
- Scissors
- Piece of outer fabric and two pieces of lining fabric the desired size of the glasses case
- Sewing machine
- Sewing thread to match fabric colour
- Hand-sewing needle

STITCHES USED

- Couching (see page 33)
- Feather stitch (see page 36)
- French knots (see page 38)
- Stem stitch (see page 44)
- Whipped wheel (see page 44)
- Woven wheel (see page 45)

THE EMBROIDERY

Using either the tracing over a light source, or dressmaker's carbon technique – depending on the fabric – (see pages 15 or 17), enlarge the design by 200 per cent and transfer onto the large piece of outer fabric, positioning it centrally. Fix the fabric into the ring frame (see page 18).

Outline the outer frame of the glasses with couching in two strands of Pearl Cotton stitched down with one strand of the same thread. Outline the inner frame with stem stitch using three strands of Stranded Cotton in colour 213.

Work the rest of the design using two strands of Stranded Cotton. Work the feather stitch along the top of the frame in colour 185. Work the jewel at the end of the feather stitch as a woven wheel with colour 185 in the middle and colour 188 as the outer edge. Work the tiny dots along the top edge as French knots in colour 1017. The largest jewel is a whipped wheel with the middle in colour 185, a band of colour 187 and the outer in colour 188. The smallest jewel is a central French knot in colour 188 surrounded by six more French knots in colour 186. The last jewel is a woven wheel in colour 186.

MAKING UP

On paper, draw out a shape to fit your sunglasses: this shape is a rectangle 20cm (8in) long by 10cm (4in) deep, with one bottom corner rounded off. Remember to add 1cm (⅜in) seam allowances all around. Cut the shape out of the paper, discarding the cut out and keeping the frame to use as a window template. Take the fabric out of the ring frame. Position the window template over the design to best effect and draw around the edge of the template with the fabric marker.

Cut out the embroidery, a back for the case and two linings, all the same shape. Pin the outer pieces right sides together. Set the sewing machine to a medium straight stitch

and, taking a 1cm (⅜in) seam allowance, sew around the case, leaving the top edge open. Press the seam stitching (not the embroidery) and clip the curves and corners. Pin the lining pieces right sides together. Taking a 1cm (⅜in) seam allowance, machine-sew down both long edges, leaving the top and bottom edges open. Press and clip as before.

Turn only the lining piece right side out. Right sides together, slip the lining into the embroidered outer and pin the layers together around the top edge.

Taking a 1cm (⅜in) seam allowance, machine-sew around the top edge. Trim the seam allowances. Pull the lining out of the outer, then turn the whole case right side out through the gap in the lining. Slip stitch the gap closed, then tuck the lining into the outer and press the top edge of the case.

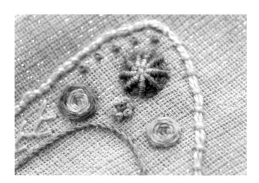

getting it right

If your sunglasses are Hollywood-huge, you might want to enlarge the design a bit so that it isn't too small on the front of your case. Make the paper pattern for the case first and see how the template looks sticky-taped to it.

Stem Stitch

Stem stitch is one of the most popular outlining stitches, and indeed, if you hold the thread to the left rather than to the right when working it, stem stitch is then renamed 'outline stitch'. It is used in the Retro Sunglasses Case (see page 42).

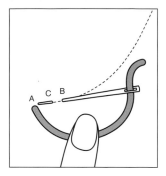

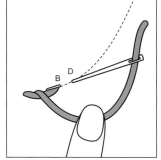

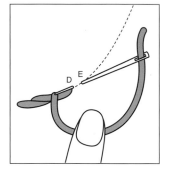

1 Bring the needle out at A at the start of the design line. Insert it at B and bring it out at C, midway between A and B, holding the thread to the right, as shown.

2 Pull the thread through to make the first stitch. Hold the working thread to the right and insert the needle at D, bringing it out at B.

3 Insert the needle at E and bring it out at D. Continue in this way, making each stitch exactly the same length.

Whipped Wheel

Whipped wheel is sometimes called ribbed wheel and can be worked to describe motifs such as flowers or snowflakes, or can be used in an abstract way in a geometric design. It is used for some of the gems in the Retro Sunglasses Case (see page 42).

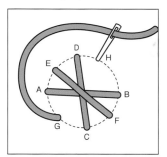

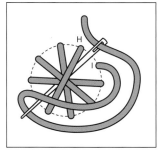

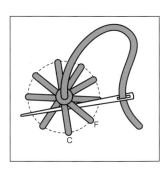

1 Bring the needle out at A and insert it at B on the other side of the circle, but slightly off-centre. Work three more straight stitches, following the sequence C–D, E–F and G–H, as shown.

2 Bring the needle out at I. Change to a blunt-tipped tapestry needle. Pass this needle under the four centre stitches without piercing the fabric. Wrap the thread over and under the needle, as shown.

3 Pull the thread taut to form a centre knot. Pass the needle under adjacent spokes F and C without piercing the fabric.

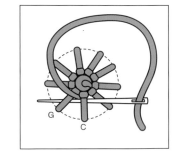

4 Pull the thread through and pass the needle over then under spoke C and under spoke G. Continue in this way around the wheel, passing the needle over and then under a spoke and under the adjacent one, until the wheel is full.

Woven Wheel

Woven wheel is sometimes called spider's web stitch and can be used in similar ways to the whipped wheel (see opposite, below). It is also used in the Retro Sunglasses Case (see page 42).

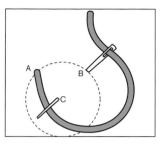

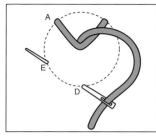

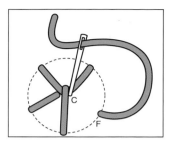

1 Bring the needle out at A and insert it at B, one-fifth of the way around the circumference of the circle. Bring the needle out at C in the centre of the circle, with the thread under the needle, as shown.

2 Insert the needle at D and bring it out at E, exactly midway between D and A.

3 Insert the needle at the side of C and then bring it out at F. Insert it at the other side of C, as shown.

4 Bring the needle out on the other side of C, right beside the spoke coming from E. Change to a blunt-tipped tapestry needle. Weave the thread under and over alternate spokes until the circle is filled.

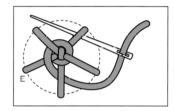

Vandyke Stitch

Vandyke stitch makes a decorative border when worked across a narrow width, as shown here. However, it can be worked across a motif such as a leaf or a wing; just follow the outer design lines and ensure that the crossed inner section remains central.

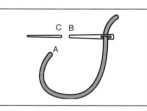

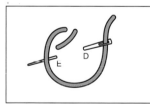

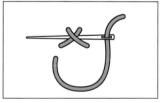

1 Bring the needle out at A on the left-hand side and take a small stitch from B to C at the top of the design area.

2 Pull the thread taut. Insert the needle at D, level with A, and bring it out at E.

3 Without piercing the fabric, pass the needle under the crossed threads, as shown.

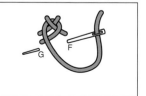

4 Pull the thread taut. Insert the needle at F, level with E, and bring it out at G.

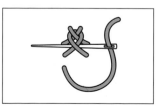

5 Repeat the sequence, passing the needle under the crossed threads immediately above until the border is finished or the shape filled.

HARDANGER

Hardanger is a form of whitework embroidery that is stitched on evenweave fabric. Though it is traditionally stitched in white thread on white fabric, coloured threads and fabrics can help to give it a contemporary twist. Thought to have originated in Persia, Hardanger gets its name from the eponymous fjord in Norway, and it's now seen as typically Scandinavian in its general style.

This form of embroidery does require careful scissor work to cut away fabric threads without damaging stitches, but it's not hard to do as long as you don't rush it.

If you are a Hardanger novice, start with the Smartphone Case (see page 56), a small project using just two stitches. Once you've understood the basic technique, move on to the Clouds Peg Bag (see page 64), though that's so pretty you may want to frame the embroidery as a picture.

Stitching Hardanger

Hardanger is worked from charted designs, so some concentration is required to count the strands accurately. However, designs are usually geometric and worked over small groups of strands, so the charts aren't tricky to follow.

For general instructions for preparing fabric, transferring a design and starting and finishing stitching, turn to pages 14–22. Below is some further information that is specific to Hardanger.

Fabrics

Hardanger must be worked on evenweave fabric (see page 8 for more details). You can buy specialist Hardanger fabric that is woven with pairs of strands separated with distinct holes that you use to make the stitches. This fabric usually has 22 strands to the inch and is stiffer than ordinary evenweave fabric. However, Hardanger fabric tends to come in very limited colours, so you can equally well use an ordinary evenweave fabric. Stitch descriptions in this chapter assume you are using Hardanger fabric and so are working over pairs of strands.

Threads

Use a fairly thick cotton pearl thread such as Anchor Pearl Cotton to stitch with. The weight of the thread needs to suit the fabric and the stitch being worked. For the kloster blocks (see opposite) the thread must cover the fabric completely, so you'll probably need Anchor Pearl Cotton no. 5 or no. 8. Some filling stitches might require a finer thread, so you can try no. 8 or no. 12. Cut short lengths – no more than 40cm (16in) – to avoid pulling the thread too many times through the fabric and spoiling its sheen and texture.

Equipment

Use a tapestry needle for Hardanger, as the blunt point will push between strands rather than splitting them. For 22-count fabric try a size 20 needle; choose a finer needle for a higher count fabric. You will need a pair of small, very sharp embroidery scissors with long narrow points for cutting away strands from the corners of kloster blocks. A pair of tweezers will be very useful for withdrawing the strands once you have cut them. You can use eyebrow tweezers, or craft ones that open when you squeeze them and close when you release your grip.

Charts

Designs are either fully charted or the repeat is charted, and the accompanying key will specify which stitch each symbol represents. If it's a repeat, tack the full size of the project onto the fabric to help you position the repeat section properly. The project charts in this book (see pages 172–173) have one grid line for each strand of evenweave fabric or each pair of strands in Hardanger fabric. Blank areas show where strands should be removed.

Starting to stitch

Use the waste knot method (see page 22) to start the thread, and finish it by weaving the end into the back of stitches. Start a new thread for each area of stitching rather than 'jumping' across the back, as long threads on the back can show through and can affect the tension of the stitches. When working any stitch that uses a single hole several times, always pass the needle down through the shared hole so any fluff is taken to the back of the work.

Kloster Blocks

Kloster blocks are rectangular blocks of satin stitch worked parallel to the fabric strands and they are the most common feature of Hardanger embroidery. All blocks must be the same size to ensure that they interlock. A block of five or seven stitches over four or six pairs of fabric strands is usual. These blocks are used in both the Smartphone Case (see page 56) and the Clouds Peg Bag (see page 64).

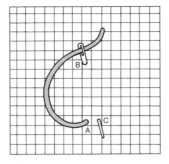

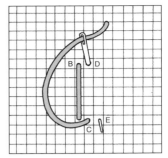

1 To work a kloster block over six pairs of strands, bring the needle out at A and insert it at B (six pairs of strands away). This forms the first of the seven satin stitches. Bring the needle out at C (one pair of strands to the side of A).

2 Insert the needle at D (one pair of strands away from B) to complete the second stitch. Bring the thread out at E (one pair of strands away from C). Continue in this way until all seven satin stitches of the kloster block have been completed.

Cutting and Withdrawing Strands

Cutting and then withdrawing strands is an essential part of Hardanger embroidery. The fabric is cut away between kloster blocks and the remaining loose strands and holes are embellished with additional stitches. The fabric strands that form the cut-away areas must be cut and removed very carefully and accurately to avoid ruining the work.

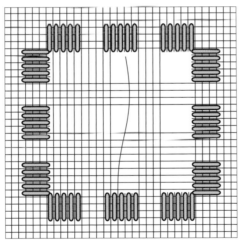

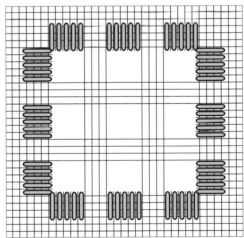

1 Work all the satin stitch embroidery surrounding the area to be cut first, because these stitches hold in place the fabric strands that are left. Ensure that all the kloster blocks (see above) surrounding an area to be cut run in the directions shown on the chart being followed.

Use small, sharp scissors with fine points to cut carefully though each pair of fabric strands next to the end of the satin stitches. Cut right up to the end of the stitches without damaging them. Strands are only cut across the end of satin stitches, not along their length. Remove the cut strands using a pair of tweezers and pulling firmly.

2 The resulting mesh can be worked on with various stitches to create the lacy effect of Hardanger embroidery. The holes can also be filled with a variety of fancy stitches.

Four-Sided Stitch

Four-sided stitch can be worked individually, in rows or in blocks. It combines well with kloster blocks (see page 49) if it is worked to the same length, creating an open square that balances the solidly stitched kloster blocks.

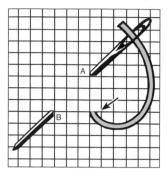 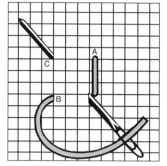 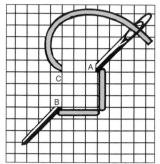

1 Bring the needle out at the lower right corner of the square to be filled (marked with an arrow). Insert the needle at the upper-right corner at A, and bring it out at B, the lower left corner and level with the starting point. For a perfect square there should be the same number of fabric strands running vertically and horizontally.

2 Insert the needle at the starting point and bring it out at C, in the upper-left corner.

3 Insert the needle at A and bring it out at B. Complete the square by inserting the needle at C. To work the next stitch to the left, bring the needle out at the lower left corner of the next square and repeat steps 2 and 3.

Snowflake Motifs

Snowflake motifs usually have eight points and a distinctly geometric design. They are worked in satin stitch blocks parallel to or diagonally across the fabric weave. Use the same thickness of thread as for any kloster blocks in the design. The central motif is used in the Smartphone Case (see page 56).

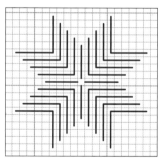 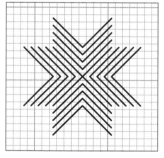 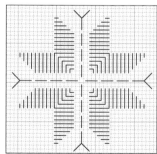

1 This tiny snowflake is made up of arrowhead-shaped blocks of satin stitch, with the stitches parallel to the weave. All the stitches are the same length and the four shapes meet at the centre.

2 As an alternative, work the same design with the stitches running diagonally across the fabric weave. Because the light catches the thread in different ways, this star takes on a two-tone appearance.

3 In this third variation the four arrowhead sections are positioned several fabric strands apart. There is decorative detail of running stitch (see page 62) and fly stitch (see page 93) between them.

Eyelet Hole Stitch

Eyelet hole stitch creates small square blocks with an eyelet hole in the middle, reminiscent of daisy flowers. The harder you pull this stitch, the larger the hole in the middle will be. The eyelet forms naturally because every stitch is worked through the central hole. Worked as a row, eyelet hole stitch makes a pretty border design.

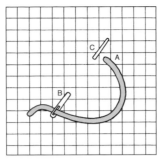

1 Bring the needle out at A, in one corner of the area to be filled. Insert the needle through the central point at B and bring it out along the outer edge of the shape to be filled at C, one pair of fabric strands away from A.

2 Continue in this way, positioning the outer ends of the stitches one pair of fabric strands apart around the edge, and always taking the thread back to the wrong side through the same central point, B.

3 The finished stitch has all the stitches radiating out from the central point.

Star Stitch

Star stitch is a simple variation of eyelet hole stitch (see above) that produces pretty stars ideal for decorating the plainer areas of a design. Each star stitch comprises eight individual stitches radiating out from a central point and can be any size.

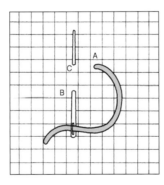

1 Bring the needle out at A in the upper-right corner of the square to be filled. Insert the needle at B in the centre of the square and bring it out midway across the upper edge of the square at C, directly above B.

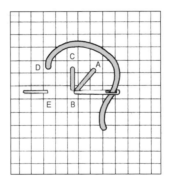

2 Take another stitch through the fabric, inserting the needle at B and bringing it out at D in the upper-left corner. Now insert the needle through the central point B and bring it out midway along the left side of the square at E, level with the central point.

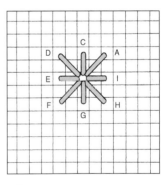

3 Insert the needle at B and bring it out at F in the lower left corner. Continue round the star, inserting the needle through the fabric at the central point and bringing it out at G, H and then I. Finish by inserting the needle at B.

Overcast Bars

Overcast bars are worked over the remaining fabric strands in areas where some strands have been removed. They are worked tightly to gather in the strands and give the finished work an airy look. Use a finer thread than for kloster blocks (see page 49). It is usually possible to use this stitch in place of any other type of bar.

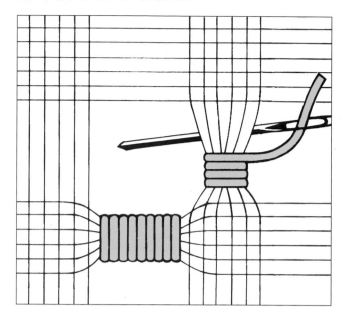

1 Bring the needle out at one end of the group of fabric strands to be covered. Pass the needle over and then under the strands and pull quite tightly to gather in the strands, as shown. Continue in this way until all the fabric strands in that section have been covered. For an even result each stitch must sit neatly next to the previous one, without overlapping. Make a note of how many stitches you used for the first bar and work the same number for all subsequent bars in the piece.

Double Overcast Bars

Double overcast bars are worked over a group of fabric strands to transform them into a pair of thin, parallel bars. Each bar should be worked over the same number of strands, so you need to begin with even-numbered groups of fabric strands. These bars are also used in the Clouds Peg Bag (see page 64).

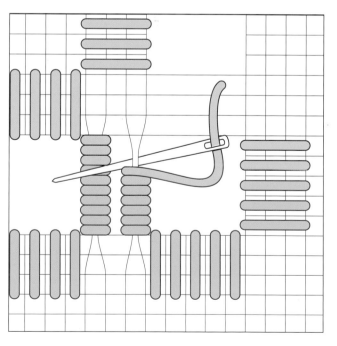

1 Select a fine thread for this stitch to ensure that the two bars will be distinct – with thick thread the bars will appear to join together. Separate the group of fabric strands into two equal sections and work an overcast bar (see above) on each one. Work the same number of stitches on each bar and remember to pull the stitches tight.

numbers of stitches

Hardanger designs are usually highly geometric so do work the same number of stitches for each bar in a pattern.

Woven Bars

Woven bars are another way of binding groups of strands. They hold the remaining fabric strands securely and add decorative detail at the same time. Use finer thread than for kloster blocks (see page 49) and maintain a firm, even tension throughout. Woven bars feature in the Clouds Peg Bag (see page 64).

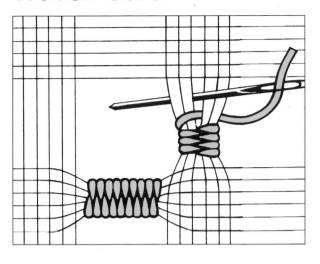

1 Bring the needle out at one end of the area to be filled. To work over four or six pairs of fabric strands, insert the needle between the second and third (or fourth and fifth) pair of fabric strands and bring it out on the other side, as shown. Repeat until the fabric strands have been completely covered with stitches. Maintain the same number of bar stitches throughout the design. If further stitches are to be worked over the cut holes, make an odd number of stitches for the woven bars because the filling stitches may need to pass under the centre stitch of each bar.

Double Woven Bars

Double woven bars create a finer effect than ordinary woven bars. They are stitched in the same way, but can only be worked over four, eight or twelve pairs of fabric strands. Choose a finer thread than for the kloster blocks (see page 49) in the design, such as Anchor Pearl Cotton no. 8, or even no. 12, depending on the desired effect.

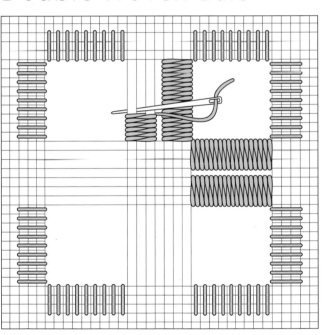

1 Separate the fabric strands for the bar into two equal groups. Work a woven bar (see above) over one set, leaving the remaining set of strands free. Work another woven bar with the same number of stitches over the remaining strands.

mix and match

Most bar stitches are interchangeable. You can add subtle variety and textural interest to your embroidery by working two or three different bars rather than using just one type. However, do plan which stitches to use and where to put them before you begin in order to maintain the geometry of the piece.

Uneven Woven Bars

Uneven woven bars are created by separating the fabric strands into three groups instead of two for a very fine, textured effect. This stitch can be worked over an even or uneven number of pairs of fabric strands.

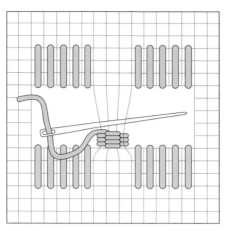

1 Bring the needle through the cut hole to the right of the fabric strands to be covered. For a group of four pairs of fabric strands, pass the needle under the second and third pair of strands only. Work the next stitch, from left to right, passing the needle under the first pair of strands, over the second and third pairs and then under the fourth pair, as shown. Continue in this way until the fabric strands are completely covered. If desired, you can work uneven woven bars in place of most other embroidered bars.

Woven Bars with Picots

Woven bars can be made more decorative and elaborate by placing picots along the edges, worked while the woven bars are being made. These protrude into the cut holes, so there is no need to work any other additional filling stitches.

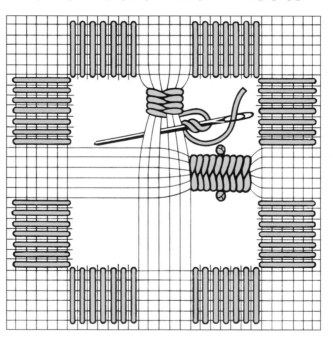

1 Begin to make a woven bar in the usual way (see page 53) but stop halfway along. Now twist the thread twice around the needle in a clockwise direction and, holding the twisted threads in place with your thumb, make the next stitch of the woven bar, as shown. The twisted thread will form a picot knot. Turn the work around so that the first picot falls along the left side of the bar and work the second picot in the same way as the first. Complete the woven bar, making sure you work the same number of stitches on each side of the picots.

Twisted Bars

Twisted bars look complicated but they are really quite straightforward. They are normally placed radiating out from the centre of a block of four cut holes, as shown, although they can also be worked diagonally across a single cut hole.

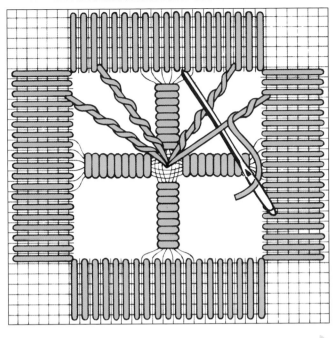

1 Work all the satin stitch, withdraw strands as required and work overcast or woven bars (see pages 52 and 53). To work a twisted bar radiating out from the centre of four cut holes, bring the needle out in the middle of the central fabric block. Insert the needle at the point where the other end of the bar is to be placed, and bring it back out through the cut hole. Take a stitch under the diagonal thread, as shown, so that the working thread is twisted around this diagonal thread. Continue until the original diagonal thread is well covered. Take the needle back to the wrong side at the original starting point and fasten off. If more twisted bars are to be worked from the same point, bring the needle back through the fabric at the starting point.

securing the bars

When the end of a twisted bar is positioned along the edge of a satin stitch block, as here, take the needle between two of the satin stitches, catching some of the fabric strands underneath. This secures it properly.

Dove's Eye Filling Stitch

Dove's eye filling stitch is a very simple filling for cut holes between groups of four kloster blocks (see page 49). It is normally worked with a finer thread than is used for the blocks. Each filling is made up of four looped stitches, each one worked around the central stitch of one of the four kloster blocks.

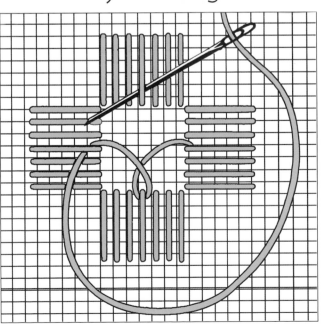

1 Bring the needle out at the left edge of the right-hand kloster block, just above the central satin stitch. Turn the fabric 90 degrees and make the next stitch under the central thread of the next kloster block, as shown. Make sure that when you pull up the thread it remains fairly loose, forming a soft loop. Continue in the same way around the hole. Pass the needle under the first looped stitch and take it back through to the wrong side at the right of the central stitch of the first kloster block.

Smartphone case

A phone left unprotected in your handbag is quickly damaged by keys and other items rattling around, but most of the cases you can buy to protect your phone are just ugly. The obvious answer is to make your own. This one uses simple Hardanger stitches in bright colours for a modern effect, and the felt lining makes the case very practical. The measurements given here are for a case that will hold a smartphone measuring 11.5 x 6cm (4½ x 2¼in).

MATERIALS

- Piece of 28-count evenweave fabric in blue-grey measuring 25 x 25cm (10 x 10in)
- 20cm (8in) ring frame
- Tape measure
- Tacking thread
- Hand-sewing needle
- Snowflake and kloster block chart (see page 172)
- Anchor Pearl Cotton no. 8: one ball in each of colours 186 and 304
- Size 24 tapestry needle
- Small, sharp scissors
- Piece of felt measuring 15 x 13cm (6 x 5in)
- Scissors
- Pins
- Sewing thread to match fabric
- Sewing machine
- Iron
- Piece of 1-cm (⅜-in)wide ribbon measuring 23cm (9in) long (optional)

STITCHES USED

- Cutting and withdrawing strands (see page 49)
- Kloster blocks (see page 49)
- Snowflake motifs (see page 50)

THE EMBROIDERY

Fix the fabric into the ring frame (see page 18). Tacking along the weave of the fabric, tack a 13 x 8cm (5 x 3in) rectangle onto the fabric, positioning it centrally (see page 16); this will be the front of the case. Starting at the top left of the tacked rectangle and using one strand of Pearl Cotton, follow the chart to work the stitch motif once, taking note of the colour sequence if you want to copy the patterning shown in the photograph (see Getting It Right, below). The lower and right-hand stars are the central two stars of the next diagonal row. The star pattern is repeated to fill the tacked rectangle, while the kloster blocks are placed at random intervals between stars.

getting it right

This embroidery uses a simple colour sequence to make the most of the pattern. The two stars on the top left are worked in colour 186 (turquoise), the next diagonal row has the outer stitch in colour 304 (orange) and the remainder in colour 186. The next row has the outer two stitches in colour 304 and the fourth and fifth rows both have the outer three stitches in colour 304. The sixth and seventh rows have the outer four stitches in colour 304, so there is just a single stitch in colour 186 in the middle of each star in these rows. The kloster blocks on the upper half of the case are worked in colour 304 while those on the lower half are worked in colour 186.

MAKING UP

Wrap the felt around the phone with the overlapped ends at centre back: a little felt will protrude top and bottom. The fit needs to be snug enough to keep the phone safe, but not so tight you can't get it easily in and out of the case. Pin the overlap in place, then oversew it.

Take the embroidered evenweave fabric out of the frame and cut it 3cm (1¼in) above the top edge and 1cm (⅜in) below the bottom edge of the stitching, but leave the side edges as they are. Fold the evenweave around the felt case, positioning the embroidery centrally on the front and allowing it to wrap around the sides a little. Arrange the fabric to meet at centre back and mark where the edges touch with pins. Remove the felt and, right sides together, pin the evenweave at the marked points. Set the sewing machine to a small straight stitch and sew the centre back seam. Set the sewing machine to a narrow, tight zigzag and zigzag the seam allowance very close to the seam stitching. Trim off all excess fabric. Arrange the fabric tube so the seam is at centre back and press it flat. Sew and zigzag the bottom seam in the same way, sewing the seam a couple of fabric strands below the edge of the embroidery. Turn the fabric case right side out, making sure the corners are pushed right out, and press it.

Matching the centre back seams, slip the felt inner into the fabric outer and slide it right down to the bottom. Turn under 5mm (¼in) around the top edge of the fabric and press, then turn all the fabric extending beyond the top of the felt to the inside, over the edge of the felt, and pin in place. On the inside, slip stitch the fabric to the felt all around. If you want a ribbon loop, tuck the ends of the ribbon under the folded-over hem and sew them in place as you slip stitch the hem.

Oblique Loop Filling Stitch

Oblique loop filling stitch can be used to fill a cut hole of almost any size. This stitch is used in the white cloud on the Clouds Peg Bag (see page 64).

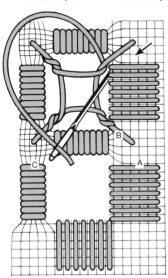

1 Bring the needle out in the centre of one of the solid fabric squares at the corner of the hole to be filled, marked by the arrow on the diagram. Insert the needle at A, in the centre of the next corner square. Leaving the thread fairly loose, bring the needle back through the cut hole at B and loop it under and around the loose thread, as shown. Insert the needle at C in the next corner and repeat the looping and twisting process. Repeat until all four sides of the stitch are complete. To finish, take the thread around the beginning of the first looped side. Take the needle through the cut hole to the wrong side and fasten off at the starting point.

Spider's Web Filling Stitch

Spider's web filling stitch can be used in the same situations as oblique loop filling stitch (see above). It produces a cross over the hole with a tiny spider's web in the centre. This pretty stitch also features in the Clouds Peg Bag (see page 64).

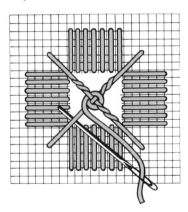

1 Begin by working a twisted bar (see page 59) diagonally across the cut hole, positioning the ends of this bar in the centre of the solid fabric squares at the corners of the hole. Now start to make another twisted bar across the same hole, using the other two corner points. Begin to work the twisting stitches around this thread until you meet the completed twisted bar at the centre point. Now darn the two diagonal bars together in an anti-clockwise direction as follows: take the needle under the first completed bar, over the unworked section of the second bar, under the other side of the first bar, over the worked section of the second bar and under the completed first bar again. Now finish the filling stitch by working the last twists around the second thread bar.

gauging the thread

The size of the hole and thickness of the thread determine how this stitch will work. Over a small hole, the stitch will only retain its lacy appearance if a very fine thread is used. But, if the area to be filled is quite large, a delicate effect can still be achieved using quite a thick thread.

Darned Wheel Filling Stitch

Darned wheel filling stitch is similar to spider's web filling stitch (see opposite, below), but can be used to fill a large cut hole. Use a finer thread than for the kloster blocks (see page 49).

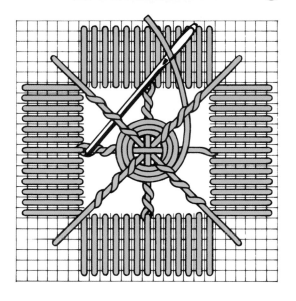

1 Work three twisted bars (see page 59) across the hole, one vertical and two diagonal. Start a fourth, horizontal bar but stop when you reach the centre where all bars meet. Working anti-clockwise around the twisted bars, take the needle under the next bar, over the next, under the next, and so on, as shown. Continue in this way until the wheel is the desired size, ending at the bar that has yet to be completed. Complete this bar and fasten off on the wrong side.

Circular Filling Stitch

Circular filling stitch looks similar to darned wheel filling stitch (see above), but with a lacier appearance. It is basically a dove's eye filling stitch (see page 55) worked over a pair of diagonal twisted bars (see page 55) with the centre darned to complete the stitch. This stitch is used in the Clouds Peg Bag (see page 64).

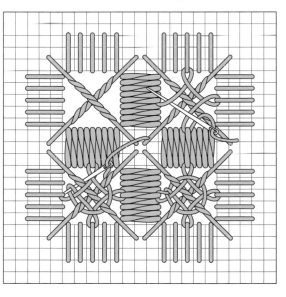

1 Work a twisted bar (see page 59) diagonally across the hole. Make a second diagonal twisted bar crossing the first, taking the thread under the first bar to link them at the centre (top-left block). Work dove's eye filling stitch (see page 59) over the same hole to the stage where the thread has been anchored to all four sides of the hole (top-right block). Now pass the thread under the first loop of the dove's eye filling stitch as though to complete it, bringing it back up at the other side of the loop. Working back around the hole, weave the needle under the twisted bars and over the dove's eye filling stitch (bottom-left block). Once you have completed a full 'round', pass the needle through the loop at the beginning of the round and take it to the back of the work (bottom-right block).

Lace Filling Stitch

Lace filling stitch can be used to fill in large areas where fabric strands have been removed; it can replace stitched bars and other filling stitches. It looks rather like dove's eye filling stitch (page 59), except that there are no stitched bars.

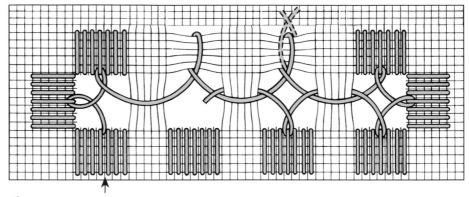

1 Work the first row of filling stitches from left to right. Bring the needle out just to the right of the central stitch in the satin stitch block below the first hole, marked by an arrow. Work two stitches around the hole as for dove's eye filling stitch. Pass the thread over the vertical fabric bar and then over and under the horizontal bar at the top of the next cut hole, bringing it out under the looped thread. Keep the thread quite loose. Continue in this way until you reach the other end of the row. Work around the end as for dove's eye filling stitch, then work back along the line of half-filled cut holes, linking the previous looped stitches, as shown. Continue in this way until you reach the original starting point and complete the first stitch. On adjacent rows work a stitch around the horizontal fabric bars to link to the stitching you have already worked on them, as shown by the dotted thread.

Ribbed Wheel Filling Stitch

Ribbed wheel filling stitch fills a square of four cut holes with a beautiful, textured design. The ribbed effect around the centre is created by winding the thread around each of the spokes of the background embroidery.

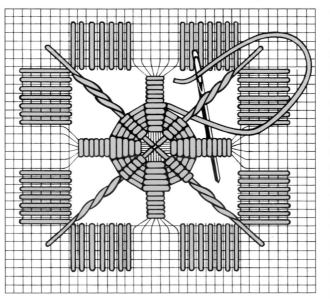

1 Work the kloster blocks and withdraw the fabric strands (see page 49) to create four holes. Work overcast bars (see page 52) over the loose strands. Work a diagonal cross of four twisted bars (see page 55) on top of this, starting and ending in the central fabric square. Bring the needle out in one of the cut holes beside the central square and pass it clockwise under one of the 'spokes' (a twisted or overcast bar). Loop the needle back under the same bar and pass it on under the next bar, as shown. Continue in this way until the wheel is the required size – usually when the stitches fall midway along the bars. Fasten off the thread behind the wheel.

Buttonhole Circle Filling Stitch

Buttonhole circle filling stitch can also be worked over a block of four cut holes. The stitches are positioned around the central solid fabric square to create a circle behind a cross, rather like a Celtic cross.

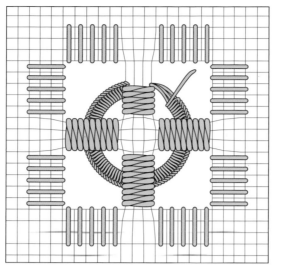

1 Work the satin stitch blocks and withdraw the necessary strands (see page 49). Work a woven bar (see page 53) over one of the four groups of fabric strands. Starting at the centre, start an adjacent woven bar over the next set of four fabric strands, stopping midway along its length at the side closest to the completed woven bar. Take a stitch through the middle of the first woven bar, then a second stitch through the half-worked bar, and a third through the same point on the completed bar, creating three strands of thread running between the two bars. Positioning the knot of each stitch on the outer edge of the arch, work back over these threads in buttonhole stitch (see page 63), ending at the half-completed bar. Finish working this woven bar.

Work half the next woven bar and then join it to the previous bar level with the end of the first arch and complete the woven bar. Work half the final woven bar. Now work two buttonholed arches, one to the left and one to the right, to complete the circle. Finish the final woven bar.

Festoon Filling Stitch

Festoon filling stitch is made up of a combination of other filling stitches, creating an ornate lacy panel. As there is quite a lot of filling work involved, it is best to use a fine thread over a fairly large block of four cut holes.

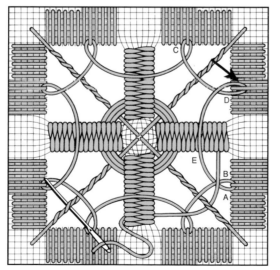

1 Work satin stitch blocks and withdraw the fabric strands (see page 49). Work woven bars (see page 53) to form the central cross. Make a diagonal twisted bar (see page 55) over each hole, radiating out from the centre. Work darned wheel filling stitch (see page 59) around the centre.

Bring the needle out halfway along one outer edge of a hole, marked on the diagram with an arrow. Working clockwise, take the thread over the woven bar and catch a satin stitch of the next block, inserting the needle at A and bringing it out at B. Continue in this way, passing the thread over each woven or twisted bar and ensuring the position of each stitch corresponds with previous ones, until you reach C. Pass the thread over the remaining twisted bar, under the first loop of thread and through the fabric at D.

Pass the needle under the stitching at the back and bring it out a few stitches along from the end of the woven bar at E. Make a final 'round' of thread loops by taking the thread over each twisted loop of the previous round and under each twisted or woven bar. When you reach the first woven bar again, fasten off the thread along the back.

Running Stitch

Running stitch is often used to separate areas of a design or to outline a motif. It creates a broken line that works well in geometrical designs. This simple stitch is used for the rain in the Clouds Peg Bag (see page 64).

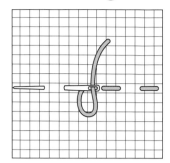

1 Bring the needle to the right side of the fabric at the start of the line. Run the needle in and out of the fabric at the given points on the chart to form a line of individual straight stitches. Usually running stitch is worked in the thickest thread used in the design, which is the same thread used for the kloster blocks (see page 49).

Hem Stitch

Hem stitch is often used in Hardanger embroidery, and was commonly a feature of the larger pieces worked in the past. The stitch is simple to work and makes a pleasant complement to the lacy effects of the filling stitches. Variations of this stitch can be found in the Drawn Thread chapter (see pages 156–169).

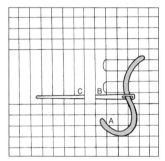

1 Remove the relevant fabric strands. Bring the needle out at A, the specified number of fabric strands below the last strand removed. Pass the needle behind the loose fabric strands in the withdrawn strand line, starting at B, directly above A. Bring the needle back out at C, the specified number of strands to the left of B.

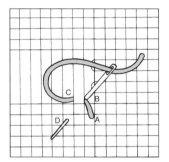

2 Insert the needle at B and bring it out directly below C and level with A at D, as shown.

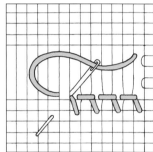

3 Continue making stitches in this way until the line is complete.

Buttonhole Stitch

Buttonhole stitch is ideal for finishing the edges of a piece of Hardanger embroidery because it can be matched to the satin stitch blocks within the design and it allows the edge to follow the design, whatever its shape. Like satin stitch, it should be worked before the fabric is cut away, but it can be worked before or after the other embroidery.

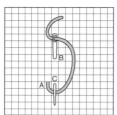 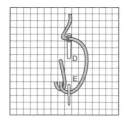 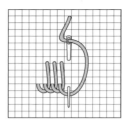 

1 Bring the needle out at A, along the outer edge of the design where the fabric will eventually be cut away. Insert the needle at B, one pair of fabric strands to the right of A and the required distance in from the 'cut' edge. Bring the needle out at C, along the 'cut' edge and directly below point B, looping the thread underneath it.

2 Make the next stitch one pair of fabric strands to the right, working in exactly the same way, inserting the needle at D and bringing it out at E.

3 Continue in this way, making each stitch exactly the same size and forming a row of little knots along the edge that will be cut.

4 At a corner insert the needle through the fabric at the same point as the previous stitch, as shown. The knot end of the stitches will still be spaced one pair of fabric strands apart, so that the stitches radiate out. Once all the stitching has been completed, trim away the excess fabric, leaving a shaped edge. Use small, sharp scissors and work from the wrong side, carefully cutting away the fabric as close to the stitches as possible without damaging them.

Squared Edging Stitch

Squared edging stitch produces a lighter, airier effect than buttonhole stitched edges and complements more open designs. It is also quicker to work than buttonhole stitch, making it a good choice over large areas.

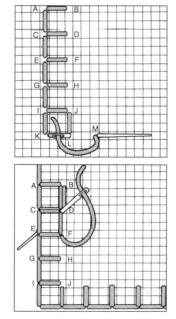

1 This stitch is worked in two stages. Work the first line before the hem is folded. Bring the needle out at A and insert it at B, bringing it out again at C. Insert the needle again at A and bring it out at C. Continue along the hemline in this way, making stitches from C to D, E to C, E to F, G to E, and so on.

2 Once this line of stitching is complete, fold the hem to the wrong side, level with the straight edge of stitching. Work the second line of stitching through both layers. Bring the needle out at D and take a stitch back to B, bringing the needle out again at D. Insert the needle at B again, bringing it out at C. Insert the needle at D. Continue in this way, making stitches from F to D twice, E to F, and so on. Once the corner is reached, trim away the excess fabric on the wrong side level with the inner line of stitching, fold in the fabric along the next edge and continue as before.

Clouds peg bag

Give a fresh look to a traditional peg bag with cloud motifs created from a selection of Hardanger stitches. This project is as easy to sew as it is charming, though if you're not handy with a saw, you'll need to enlist a tiny bit of help in this project, as the wooden coat hanger needs to be cut down to fit in the peg bag.

MATERIALS

- Piece of 22-count Hardanger fabric measuring 30 x 30cm (12 x 12in)
- 25cm (10in) ring frame
- Tape measure
- Cloud charts (see page 172)
- Anchor Pearl Cotton no. 5: one ball in each of colours 2 and 158
- Size 26 tapestry needle
- Piece of medium-weight plain cotton fabric measuring 30 x 30cm (12 x 12in)
- Wooden coat hanger
- Fading fabric marker
- Scissors
- Pins
- Sewing thread to match fabric
- Sewing machine
- Piece of medium-weight printed cotton fabric measuring 30 x 12cm (12 x 4¾in) and piece measuring 30 x 22cm (12 x 8¾in)

STITCHES USED

- Cutting and withdrawing strands (see page 49)
- Double overcast bars (see page 52)
- Kloster blocks (see page 49)
- Oblique loop filling stitch (see page 58)
- Running stitch (see page 62)
- Spider's web filling stitch (see page 58)
- Woven bars (see page 53)

THE EMBROIDERY

The embroidery can be positioned anywhere on the Hardanger fabric, as long as it is at least 2.5cm (1in) in from the sides, 3cm (1¼in) up from the bottom and 6cm (2¾in) down from the top. Fix the fabric into the ring frame (see page 18). Following the charts and using one strand of Pearl Cotton, embroider the white cloud using colour 2. Work the bars defining the blocks on the left of the cloud as woven bars and those on the right as double overcast bars. Embroider the blue cloud using colour 158. Under each cloud, work slanting lines of running stitch with the stitches varying in length from two to four threads, and the gaps between them two or three threads.

MAKING UP

Use a saw to cut the wooden coat hanger down to 27cm (10½in) wide (measured from tip of arm straight across to tip of other arm); sand the end smooth. Lay the plain cotton fabric flat; position the coat hanger on it with the wooden bar on the top edge and the hook centred left to right. Draw along the curves of the top of the wooden bar and cut the fabric to shape. Pin the right side of the plain fabric to the back of the embroidery and cut the top edge of the embroidered fabric to match. With the layers still pinned, set the sewing machine to a narrow zigzag stitch and sew the fabrics together around the edges; this will be the back of the bag.

Cut the top of the small rectangle of printed fabric to the same shape as the top of the back piece. Turn under a double 1cm (⅜in) hem on the long straight edge and press it. Turn under and press the same hem on one long edge of the other piece of print fabric. Fold out both hems and pin the pieces together along the second fold line. Set the sewing machine to a medium straight stitch and machine-sew along the fold line for 5cm (2in), then reverse to secure the stitching. Repeat from the other side, so that the pieces are joined at the sides with a 20cm (8in) gap in the middle (this is where you put the pegs into the bag). Refold the hems, pin and then machine-sew them close to the lower edges.

Right sides facing, pin the joined fabric front piece to the embroidered back, matching the outer edges. Taking a 1cm (⅜in) seam allowance, sew around the edges, leaving a 1cm (⅜in) gap at top centre for the coat hanger hook. Zigzag the edges together and trim them. Turn right side out and press. Insert the coat hanger.

BLACKWORK

Based on repeated geometric motifs and patterns, this style of counted thread embroidery has Moorish origins dating back many centuries. However, the abstract nature of the patterns has kept them fresh and they look as good in a contemporary embroidery as they do in a Tudor one.

The range and versatility of the 30 patterns given here mean that a completely novice embroiderer can easily produce something lovely using a single stitch pattern, such as the Blackwork Buttons (see page 76). As the patterns are easy and therapeutic to stitch (you just have to be able to count!), progressing to combining several patterns in one project is a small step; try the Bird Book Bag (see page 82).

From these projects it's an easy move to creating your own original pieces using the patterns that appeal most.

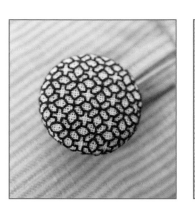 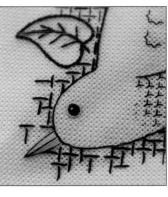  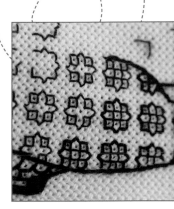

Stitching Blackwork

The shading effects that are typical of blackwork pictures are achieved in three ways. Firstly, by changing the pattern: a denser pattern makes for a darker effect and vice versa; you'll find notes with patterns advising on how best to use them. Secondly, patterns can be worked in different threads (see below) to make thicker and so more visually dense lines. Thirdly, you can break up patterns by missing out stitches to create a gradual lightening effect in an area. The Bird Book Bag (see page 82) shows these techniques well.

For general instructions for preparing fabric, transferring a design and starting and finishing stitching, turn to pages 14–22. Below is some further information that is specific to blackwork.

Fabrics

Blackwork was traditionally worked on white or off-white linen. You can work on any evenweave fabric (see page 8 for more details), and the most popular blackwork fabrics today are Aida and evenweave linen.

Aida is made from 100 per cent cotton and is woven in regular, clearly defined blocks to make stitching very easy. The sizes of these blocks determine the size of the stitching. Aida is generally available in counts of 7, 10, 11, 12, 14, 16, 18 and 22. Most blackwork stitches will be worked over one block of Aida, so if you use 11-count you will fit 11 stitches on one inch of the fabric, each worked over one block; if you use 22-count you will be able to work 22 stitches over one inch of fabric. The finer the fabric, the more delicate the design, but if you are new to blackwork, try starting with a 14- or 16-count Aida.

Evenweave fabric is available in higher stitch counts (28 and 32 are common), but you work over two strands rather than one block. So a 28-count evenweave will give you 14 stitches to an inch, the same as 14-count Aida.

Threads

Anchor Stranded Cotton is a high-quality stranded 100 per cent mercerised cotton thread that has six strands (see page 10 for more details). You can use one or two strands for blackwork, depending on how thick you want the line to be.

Anchor Coton à Broder is 100 per cent mercerised soft cotton. It comes in various thicknesses (called 'tickets') and in this book ticket no. 16 (the most popular thickness) has been used. You only use one strand of this thread.

Needle

Use a tapestry needle when working on either Aida or evenweave fabric so that you push between the fabric strands rather than piercing them. For stitching on a 14-count fabric, use a number 24 tapestry needle.

Charts

Like all counted thread work, blackwork is stitched from a chart. Patterns are worked over one block of Aida or two strands of evenweave unless otherwise stated: so one square in the charts given represents one block of Aida or two strands of evenweave. Patterns can be partly worked to make an area gradually lighter in tone; to do this you just work increasingly smaller sections of the pattern, keeping the spacing of the missing sections consistent. The broken patterns can be quite freeform or more regular, whatever suits the design. In these charts each new stage of stitching is shown by red lines, with blue lines indicating stitches made at previous stages.

Starting to stitch

Use the waste knot method (see page 22) to start the thread and finish it by weaving the end into the back of stitches. You can 'jump' across the back of the fabric a short distance to start a new motif; unless you are using a very fine fabric the dark thread will not show through.

If areas of a project have outlines, these are worked first in backstitch (see page 23) or stem stitch (see page 44), or double running stitch, and then the filling patterns are added. For double running stitch you work a line in running stitch (see page 23) and then work back along the line, filling in the gaps.

Pattern 1

Pattern 1 is a small design that creates a series of squares. It is quite dense and so can be very useful for creating depth in a design.

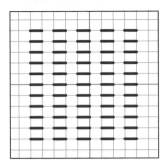

1 Start the pattern at the top right and work a row of horizontal running stitches from right to left. Work the next line from left to right, then back again from right to left, and so on until the area is filled.

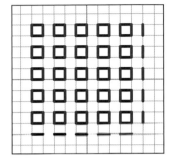

2 Work rows of vertical running stitches with the same spacing, positioning the stitches to share holes with the horizontal stitches to create small squares. Work the first row from bottom to top, the second from top to bottom, and so on.

Pattern 2

Pattern 2 is a simple variation of the previous pattern that is worked in the same way. It offers a less uniform look that is still fairly dense.

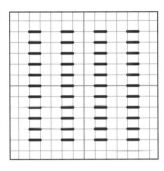

1 Start the pattern at the top right and work a row of horizontal running stitches from right to left. Work each stitch over one block of Aida (two strands of evenweave fabric), but space the stitches two blocks of Aida (four strands of evenweave) apart. Work the next line from left to right, then back again from right to left, and so on until the whole area is filled.

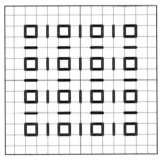

2 Work rows of vertical running stitches in the same sequence as the horizontal stitches. They should combine with the horizontal stitches to create a series of squares and dashes. Work the first row from bottom to top, the second row from top to bottom, and so on.

Pattern 3

Pattern 3 is another small pattern; it creates a series of open crosses that fill up a large area quite quickly.

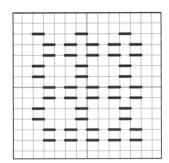

1 Starting at the top right of the area to be filled, work horizontal running stitches in the pattern shown. Work from right to left, then left to right and back again until the area is covered.

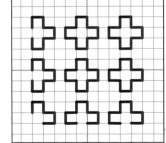

2 Work the vertical stitches in rows as shown, working from top to bottom, then bottom to top, and so on.

Pattern 4

Pattern 4 creates a simple basketwork effect that can be very useful in pictorial designs for areas such as roofs and walls. It is one of the more masculine-looking stitches and will fill a large area quickly.

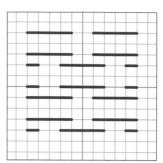

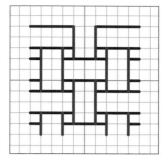

1 Start at top right of the area to be filled and work sets of four horizontal stitches from right to left, then left to right over four blocks of Aida (eight strands of evenweave), with two blocks (four strands) between each set. Space these rows two blocks (four strands) apart. Leave one block (two strands) and work rows 3 and 4 in the staggered arrangement shown. Repeat to fill the area.

2 Now work the vertical stitches in the same sequence as before to produce a woven look.

Pattern 5

Pattern 5 is a variation of pattern 4, but is lighter and more delicate. It is a versatile pattern as it can be used for filling large areas quickly, and also works on a small scale.

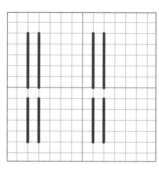

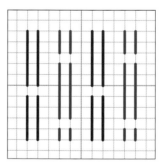

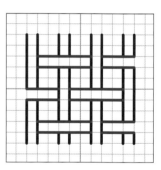

1 Starting at the top right, work a set of five vertical stitches over five blocks of Aida (ten strands of evenweave). Miss one block (two strands), and work the next set. Repeat one block, or two strands, to the left. Then miss five blocks (ten strands) and repeat to work a second pair. Continue in this way.

2 Work further sets of vertical stitches between the existing vertical stitches in a staggered formation, as shown.

3 Now work the horizontal stitches to create the basketwork effect, working from right to left on the top row, then left to right on the next row and so on.

Pattern 6

Pattern 6 is a variation of pattern 4 that is worked on the diagonal. It is useful for describing obviously sloping areas, such as roofs.

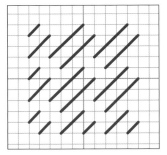 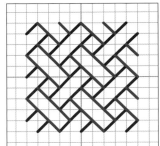

1 Start at the top right and work sets of diagonal stitches towards the bottom left, as shown.

2 Work the stitches on the opposite diagonal, this time starting at the bottom right.

Pattern 7

Pattern 7 is a simplified version of the previous pattern that creates a more open look. It is used as the background pattern for the Bird Book Bag (see page 82).

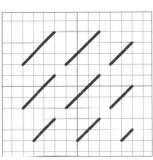 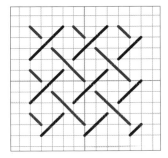

1 Start at the top right and work long sets of diagonal stitches from top right to bottom left.

2 Now work diagonal stitches from bottom right to top left to finish the quilted pattern.

mix and match

Patterns that are worked on the diagonal, like the ones on this page, have their own rhythm that can help to break up the regularity of square-based blackwork patterns. Use these diagonal patterns to add extra visual variety to your projects.

Pattern 8

Pattern 8 is a simple diamond pattern that is one of the most useful and easiest pattern stitches of all.

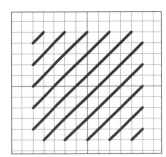 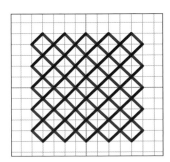

1 Work lines of diagonal backstitches from top right to bottom left.

2 Repeat, this time working from bottom right to top left, creating the diamond pattern.

Pattern 9

Pattern 9 is an old pattern – dating back to the Tudor period – that is very useful for filling oddly shaped areas. Because it is so small, it looks very dark, though it is very easy to work. This stitch is used for one of the Blackwork Buttons (see page 76).

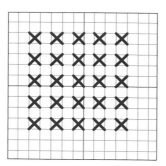 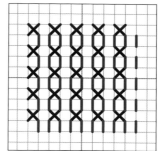 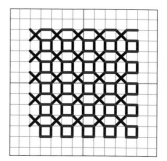

1 Starting at the top right, work vertical columns of cross stitches.

2 Work vertical columns of running stitches between the cross stitches. Work the first column from top to bottom, the next from bottom to top, and so on.

3 Now work rows of horizontal running stitches in the same way to complete the pattern.

Pattern 10

Pattern 10 is a simple pattern that creates an open trellis effect. It is delicate without being overly feminine.

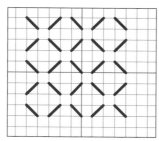 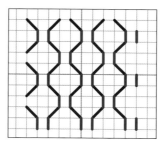 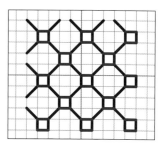

1 Starting at the top right, work zigzag stitches to the left, then work back to the right with the zigzags running in the opposite direction.

2 Work running stitches in vertical columns to join the zigzags, as shown.

3 Finally work horizontal rows of running stitch in the same formation to complete the pattern.

Pattern 11

Pattern 11 is similar to the previous pattern and is another very old pattern. Again, the effect is quite dense.

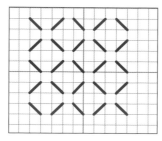 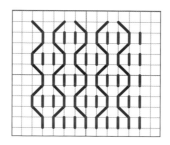 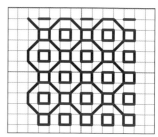

1 Work zigzag rows of running stitch as for pattern 10.

2 Work vertical columns of running stitch to join and in between the zigzags, as shown.

3 Now work rows of horizontal running stitches in the same way to complete the pattern.

Pattern 12

Pattern 12 forms a pretty honeycomb effect. It is especially good for small, straight-sided areas.

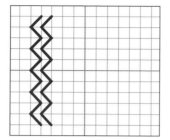 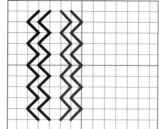 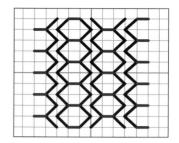

1 Starting at the top of the design area, work two identical vertical rows of zigzags, as shown.

2 Leave one vertical row of Aida blocks (two strands of evenweave) to the right and work two more rows of zigzags as a mirror image. Repeat to fill the area.

3 Working from right to left on the top row and then from left to right on the next row, work horizontal rows of stitches, joining the points of the zigzags.

Pattern 13

Pattern 13 is the archetypal honeycomb pattern. It is easy to work and has a light and lacy effect.

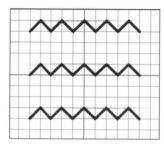 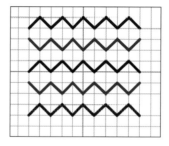 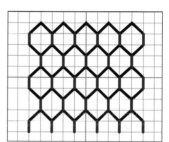

1 Start at the top right and work horizontal rows of zigzags spaced three blocks of Aida (six strands of evenweave) apart, as shown.

2 Between the first rows, work further rows of zigzag stitches, this time in mirror image.

3 Work vertical lines of running stitch from top to bottom on the first row – then from bottom to top, and so on – to join the zigzags into a honeycomb trellis.

Pattern 14

Pattern 14 is a variation of the honeycomb pattern and is also useful for filling small areas. Take care when working stage two to make the zigzag lines run in the right directions.

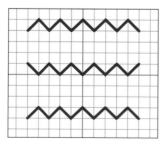 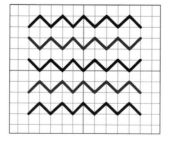 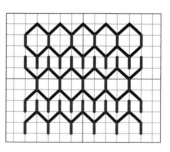

1 Starting at the top right, work rows of zigzag stitches with the directions of the zigzags alternating, as shown.

2 Now fill in the alternate rows of zigzag stitches, taking care that these are positioned exactly as shown.

3 Work vertical lines of running stitches from top to bottom then bottom to top and so on, following the formation shown.

Pattern 15

Pattern 15 is another variation of the honeycomb pattern. This pattern is used for one of the Blackwork Buttons (see page 76).

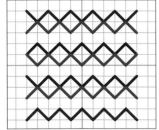 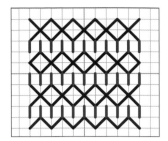 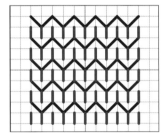

1 Start at the top right and work rows of zigzag stitches in alternating directions, as shown.

2 Work further rows of zigzag stitches, also in alternating directions, to form crosses and diamonds.

3 Work vertical rows of running stitch so the stitches appear between the crosses and diamonds, as shown.

Pattern 16

Pattern 16 is similar to the previous patterns and is a useful pattern for covering small areas that need to be quite densely filled.

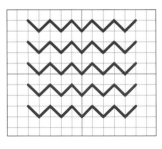 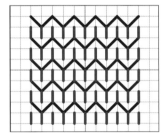

1 Starting at the top right, work a horizontal row of zigzag stitches. Work further rows with the zigzags all going in the same direction.

2 Starting at the top right and working from top to bottom, then bottom to top, add vertical rows of running stitch, as shown.

Pattern 17

Pattern 17 creates a series of angled V shapes that overlap, rather like feathers, making it ideal for the tail of the bird on the Bird Book Bag (see page 82).

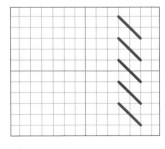 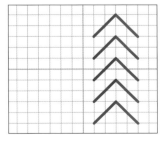 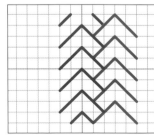

1 Start the pattern at the top right and work sets of two joined diagonal stitches.

2 Working from bottom to top, work a second line of diagonal stitches to form large, upside down Vs, as shown.

3 Work a second set of Vs with each one starting halfway along the previous stitches. Repeat to fill the area.

Pattern 18

Pattern 18 works well on a medium-sized, irregular area. It is easy to construct and creates an open and bold trellis pattern that is used for one of the Blackwork Buttons (see page 76).

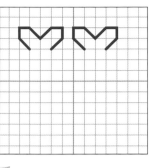

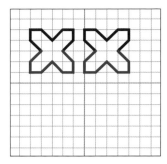

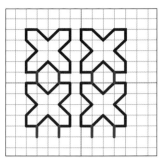

1 Start at the top right and work the top half of the cross shapes, moving across towards the left.

2 Work back across the row from left to right, filling in the bottom half of the crosses. Repeat to fill the area.

3 Starting at the top right, work columns of vertical running stitches to join the open crosses, working from top to bottom on the first column, then bottom to top, and so on.

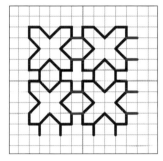

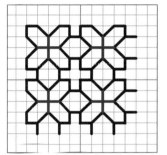

4 Repeat to work rows of horizontal running stitches, working the first row from right to left, the second from left to right, and so on.

5 Work a vertical cross inside each open cross, working each arm of the cross over one block of Aida (two strands of evenweave).

Pattern 19

Pattern 19 is geometrically elegant and visually light. This pattern is used for the bird's breast feathers in the Bird Book Bag (see page 82).

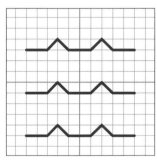

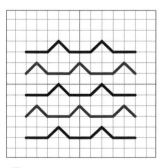

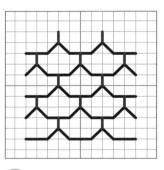

1 Starting at the top right, work two backstitches to the left, one diagonally upwards, and one diagonally down. Repeat across the fabric. Work further rows four blocks of Aida (eight strands of evenweave) apart.

2 Repeat these rows between the existing rows, but offset them to the left by two blocks of Aida (four strands of evenweave) as shown.

3 Work vertical columns of stitches, as shown, to join the horizontal rows.

Blackwork buttons

As buttons are so small and quick to stitch, they offer the perfect opportunity for testing out patterns and practising technique, and you can choose almost any of the patterns in this chapter. One of these buttons is in red, a colour sometimes used in antique blackwork textiles. Many blackwork patterns look amazing in coloured thread, so do experiment with your favourite colours and patterns.

MATERIALS

- Piece of blackwork linen large enough to accommodate all the buttons you want to make
- 29mm (⅛in) self-cover button kit
- Pencil
- Ring frame to fit fabric
- Anchor Stranded Cotton: one skein in each of colours 403 and 1005
- Size 10 embroidery needle
- White, lightweight fusible interfacing (optional)
- Iron

PATTERNS USED

- Pattern 15 (see page 74)
- Pattern 18 (see page 75)
- Pattern 26 (see page 80)

THE EMBROIDERY

Using the template provided with the button kit and a pencil, draw a circle for each button needed onto blackwork linen. Fix the fabric into a ring frame (see page 18).

Starting at the centre of a circle, work the chosen pattern using two strands of black, or red, Stranded Cotton. Work the pattern across and outwards to one edge – stopping a few millimetres from the pencil line – then return to the centre and work out in another direction until the whole circle is filled.

MAKING UP

When all the circles are embroidered, take the linen out of the frame. As the linen is thin, if you have a metal button kit you may need to back the embroidery to stop the metal showing through: if the kit is white plastic this won't be necessary. To back the embroidery, cut a circle of fusible interfacing with a 1.5cm (⅝in) radius for each button. Following the manufacturer's instructions, iron a circle of interfacing into the middle of each embroidered circle. Don't iron the interfacing over the whole of the embroidered circle as this makes the fabric quite thick and then it becomes difficult to snap the back onto the button without damaging it.

Carefully cut out each embroidered circle along the pencil line. Following the instructions on the button kit, use one embroidered circle to cover each button.

getting it right

The buttons should not be washed or dry-cleaned, so they are best used on a coat or other item that doesn't need frequent laundering. However, they are very quick to sew on, so it's easy to snip them off for occasional cleaning, then sew them on again.

Pattern 20

Pattern 20 shows how you can take a basic motif and turn it into an all-over design. This pattern is intricate-looking and works well in a large area.

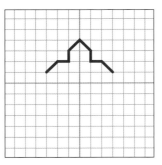

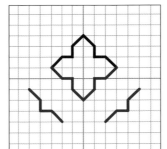

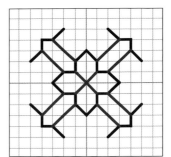

1 Start at the top right and work the top half of a motif. Leave a gap of four blocks of Aida (eight strands of evenweave), and work the top of a second motif. Continue in the same way across the fabric.

2 Working back from left to right, stitch the bottom half of each motif. On the next row work back across the fabric, stitching the top half of the next row of motifs. Space them between the motifs of the previous row as shown. Continue in this way to fill the area.

3 Work a cross made up of four diagonal stitches in the centre of each motif. Then work diagonal lines of backstitch to join the motifs, as shown, working each backstitch over one block of Aida (two strands of evenweave).

Pattern 21

Pattern 21 uses the same central motif as the previous pattern, but to very different effect.

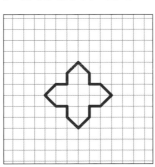

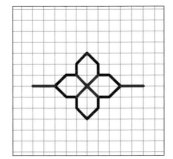

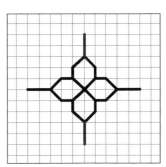

mixing motifs

It can be interesting to use patterns with the same motif together in a project, but be careful that the design doesn't become visually confused, making it difficult to differentiate between areas.

1 Work stages one and two of pattern 20, fleaving four blocks of Aida (eight strands of evenweave) between each motif.

2 Work a cross made up of four diagonal stitches in the centre of each motif. Then work horizontal lines of backstitch linking each motif in each row.

3 Finally work vertical lines of backstitch to link columns of motifs.

Pattern 22

Pattern 22 has a spacious feel and is ideal for a large area that does not want to look visually cramped.

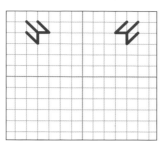

1 Start at the top right and work the bottom quarters or halves of each star in the top row, depending on the space (quarters are shown here). Leave six blocks of Aida (12 strands of evenweave) between each one.

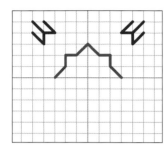 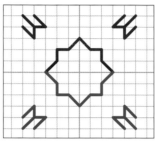 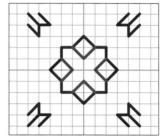 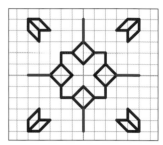

2 Work back across the row, stitching the top half of each large motif, as shown.

3 Work a third row, completing the lower half of each large motif, then start the stars and continue in the same way.

4 Fill the centre of the large motifs with Vs made of two stitches, positioning them as shown.

5 Work vertical lines of backstitch to join the large motifs. Then work horizontal lines of backstitch to complete the design.

Pattern 23

Pattern 23 features the central motif used in the previous pattern, but filled in in a different way. The wing of the bird on the Bird Book Bag (see page 82) is worked in this pattern.

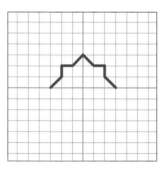 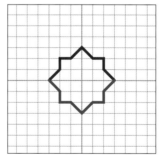 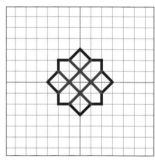

1 Starting at the top right, work the top half of a motif. Leave a gap of four blocks of Aida (eight strands of evenweave), and repeat the motif across the fabric.

2 Work back across the area, filling in the lower half of each motif. Repeat these stages to fill the area, leaving a gap of four blocks (eight strands) between rows.

3 Work diagonal lines of backstitch, working each stitch over one block (two strands) to fill the motif with a trellis.

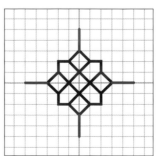

4 Work horizontal rows of backstitch to join motifs and then work vertical rows to complete the pattern, again working each stitch over one block (two strands).

Pattern 24

Pattern 24 shows how you can combine two motifs to create a whole new design. Here the motif from pattern 23 is combined with a snowflake motif to make a very pretty pattern suitable for large areas of a design.

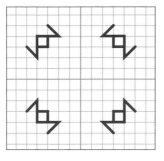

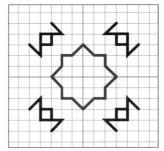

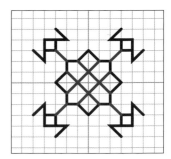

1 Starting at the top right, work the bottom quarter or half of each snowflake motif, depending on space, positioning them as shown (quarters are shown here). Leave a gap of four blocks of Aida (eight strands of evenweave) and work the top of the next row of snowflakes. Continue in this way to fill the area.

2 Working from right to left, stitch the top half of each central motif, positioning these motifs between the snowflakes. Fill in the lower half of the motifs on the return journey.

3 Work trellis in the motif as in step 3 of pattern 23, adding the stitches that join the central motifs to the snowflakes.

Pattern 25

Pattern 25 is a bold pattern that can cover a medium to large area quite quickly, and is easier to stitch than it might appear.

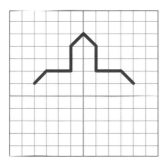

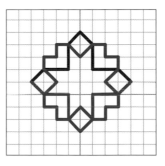

1 Starting at the top right, work the shape shown. Leave two blocks of Aida (four strands of evenweave) and work another half motif. Repeat across the fabric.

2 On the return journey complete the lower half of this element of the motif. Work further rows spaced two blocks of Aida (four strands of evenweave) apart. Work the second element of the motif in the same way.

3 Work the outline motifs, as shown. Then work the central cross in each motif, using backstitch and working each stitch over one block of Aida (two strands of evenweave).

4 Finally, work the diagonal lines across the outline motifs, as shown, again using backstitch.

Pattern 26

Pattern 26 is a very pretty, dainty little pattern that looks like a scattering of flowers or stars across a medium or large area. It is used for one of the Blackwork Buttons (see page 76), and can also be used as a border.

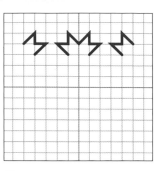

1 Starting at the top right and working towards the left, stitch the top half of a row of stars.

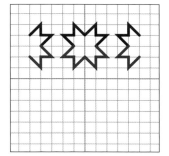

2 On the return journey, work the lower half of each star.

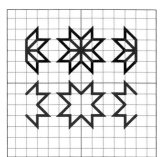

3 Work further rows of stars to fill the area. Work a double cross in the centre of each star.

Pattern 27

Pattern 27 is a variation of the previous pattern. The stars are joined with backstitches to create a completely new, denser pattern.

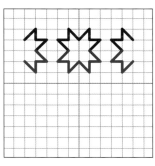

1 Work a series of stars in the same way as for pattern 26. Work further rows, positioning each row one block of Aida (two strands of evenweave) apart.

2 Work diagonal lines of backstitch to join the stars, as shown. Work each stitch over one block of Aida (two strands of evenweave).

3 Work a vertical cross in the centre of each star, working first the horizontal stitches in each row and then the vertical ones.

Pattern 28

Pattern 28 is a simple diamond design that looks good in fairly regularly shaped areas. Each backstitch is worked over one block of Aida (two strands of evenweave).

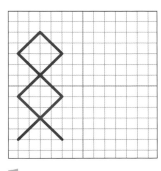

1 Starting at the top, work a backstitched zigzag line towards the bottom. Work back up in mirror image.

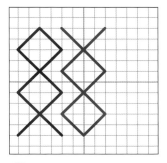

2 Work another row of diamonds, offset by two blocks of Aida (four strands of evenweave), as shown.

3 Continue in this way to fill the area. Then work the crosses in each diamond.

Pattern 29

Pattern 29 is a more complicated version of the previous pattern that combines alternate rows of diamonds and zigzags. With this pattern, it is important to work in the suggested order, as you can go wrong fairly easily.

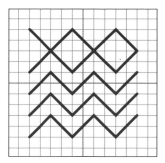

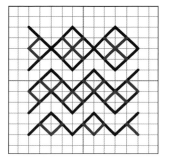

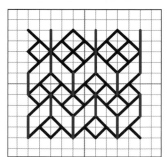

1 Starting at the top right, stitch a horizontal row of diamonds, two rows of zigzags and then a row of diamonds, as shown. Continue this pattern to fill the area. (In this chart the bottom zigzag row is the start of the second diamond row.)

2 Fill in the diamonds with backstitch crosses. Join each pair of zigzag lines with single stitches, in the pattern shown.

3 Now, work vertical lines of backstitch to join the rows of diamonds and crosses.

Pattern 30

Pattern 30 is made out of a single motif that alternates its position on different rows. You can join up the open crosses by extending the vertical and horizontal running stitches.

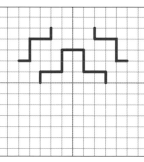

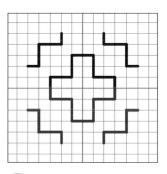

1 Starting at the top right, work the lower half of a line of open crosses, placing each one four blocks of Aida (eight strands of evenweave) apart. Work back across, working the top half of the crosses in the line below, placing these centrally between those of the previous row.

2 Continue to work in this way to fill the area.

3 Work double crosses at the centre of each motif, as shown.

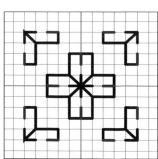

4 Work the vertical stitches at the end of each arm of each cross, then work the horizontal stitches.

Bird book bag

This easy-to-make book bag features an enquiring bird embroidered in blackwork. The filling patterns are worked in different threads to create the shading that is a feature of blackwork portraits and figures.

MATERIALS

- Piece of 20-count evenweave linen measuring 45 x 45cm (18 x 18in)
- Tacking thread
- Hand-sewing needle
- Bird template (see page 170)
- Tissue paper
- Anchor Coton à Broder ticket 16: one skein in black
- Anchor Stranded Cotton: one skein in each of colours 403 and 305
- Size 10 embroidery needle
- Two pieces of 20-count evenweave linen measuring 35 x 35cm (14 x 14in)
- Pins
- Sewing thread to match fabric colour
- Sewing machine
- Fading fabric marker
- Two pieces of 20-count evenweave linen measuring 40 x 6cm (16 x 2½in)
- Two pieces of 3-cm (1¼-in) wide grosgrain ribbon measuring 40cm (16in) long
- Piece of 20-count evenweave linen measuring 68 x 10cm (26¾ x 4in)

PATTERNS USED

- Pattern 7 (see page 71)
- Pattern 17 (see page 74)
- Pattern 19 (see page 75)
- Pattern 23 (see page 78)
- Satin stitch (see page 40)
- Stem stitch (see page 44)

THE EMBROIDERY

Fix the largest square of fabric into a slate frame (see page 19). Tacking along the weave of the fabric, tack a 35 x 35cm (14 x 14in) square onto the fabric, positioning it centrally. Enlarge the template by 200 per cent. Using the tacking technique (see page 16), transfer the bird design onto the fabric, positioning it where you want, but at least 5cm (2in) in from the edges of the tacked square.

Outline the bird in stem stitch, using two strands of Coton à Broder from the dotted line on the neck around to the dotted line on the chest, and from the back of the wing around to the dotted line on the wing. Use stem stitch and one strand to complete the outlining. Embroider the beak in satin stitch with two strands of Stranded Cotton in colour 305 and outline it with a single strand of Stranded Cotton in colour 403. Outline the eye with stem stitch in two strands of colour 305 and fill it with

more stem stitch in two strands of colour 403, leaving a tiny piece of plain fabric as a highlight.

Embroider the leaves in stem stitch using two strands of Coton à Broder. Work the thighs in satin stitch and the lower legs in three rows of stem stitch, using two strands of Stranded Cotton in colour 403 throughout.

Using the photograph as a guide for stitch position, embroider the tail with pattern 17, starting with two strands of Stranded Cotton in colour 403 and changing to one strand as the pattern breaks up (see page 68). Embroider the wing with pattern 23, using the same thread as for the tail. Start with two strands, change to one strand, then break up the pattern. For the breast, use pattern 19, starting it with two strands of Coton à Broder then changing to one strand and finally breaking up the pattern. Fill in around the head and body with pattern 7, using one or two strands of Coton à Broder to change weight as required.

MAKING UP

Take the fabric out of the frame and cut it along the tacked lines. Lay one square piece of fabric flat, lay the embroidered piece face down on top, and the remaining piece on top of that, matching all edges. Set the sewing machine to a medium straight stitch. Taking a 1.5cm (⅝in) seam allowance, sew one side, across the bottom, and up the other side. Set the machine to a medium zigzag stitch and neaten the seam allowances.

Separating the layers so the embroidered front has two layers (protecting the back of the embroidery from shopping) and the back one layer, flatten one bottom corner so the seams touch and put in a pin. From the corner, measure 2cm (¾in) along a seam. Using the fabric marker, draw a line across the corner at right angles to the seam. Machine-sew along the line. Hand-sew the tip of the corner to the bottom seam allowance. Repeat on the opposite corner.

Fold both long edges of each 6cm (2½in) handle strip towards the middle and press to make strips 3cm (1¼in) wide. Pin, then tack the ribbons to the folded strips, matching the long edges. Thread the sewing machine to match the ribbon on the top spool and to match the fabric on the bobbin and set it

to a medium straight stitch. Sew along the very edges of each ribbon to sew them to the fabric. Remove the tacking stitches.

Right sides together, pin the ends of a handle to the front top edge of the bag, so the raw edges match and the handle hangs down the bag face. Position each end 7cm (2¾in) from a side seam. Repeat with the other handle on the bag back.

The final piece of fabric will be the facing at the top. Zigzag stitch one long edge, then turn under and sew a narrow hem. Leaving a 1.5cm (⅝in) seam allowance and starting at a side seam, pin the facing right sides together around the top of the bag. When it is pinned on, take out the first and last pins and pin the short ends of the facing together. Taking a 1.5cm (⅝in) seam allowance, sew this seam then zigzag stitch it. Pin the loose facing to the bag again. Taking a 1.5cm (⅝in) seam allowance, sew the facing to the top edge. Sew around twice – the second time just below the first line – and on the second line, reverse and sew forwards again over the end of each handle. Zigzag stitch then trim the seam allowance. Turn the facing to the inside of the bag and press the top edge. If you wish, you can machine-sew the bottom edge of the facing to the inside of the bag.

CREWELWORK

Dating back to at least the 11th century, crewelwork is a form of embroidery still much-loved today. The Bayeux Tapestry is the earliest surviving example of crewelwork (despite the name it is an embroidery, not a woven tapestry), though the designs we now think of as traditional in crewelwork – exotic, stylised animals, trees, flowers, insects and birds – date from the 1600s, the Jacobean period.

There are a multitude of stitches to experiment with, so you can start with simple stitches such as chain and stem stitch and make the glamorous Sleeping Mask (see page 94). The Flora Bolster (see page 104) is a contemporary interpretation of Jacobean motifs and uses a wider range of stitches, but a little practice of any unfamiliar ones will show you that none of them are really tricky to work.

Turn to pages 14–23 for general instructions for preparing fabric, transferring a design, and stitching.

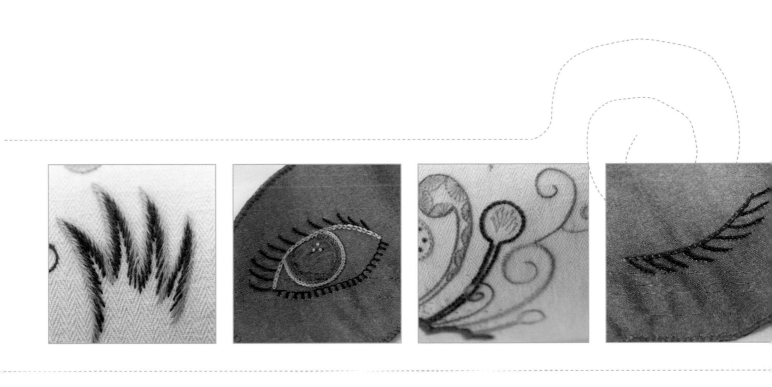

Battlement Couching

Battlement couching
is a decorative filling
that is traditionally
worked in four tones
of one colour from
light to dark, or vice
versa. In the diagrams
here the colours
are quite different
for clarity, but you
can choose subtly
changing shades.

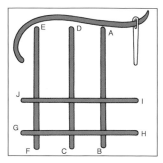 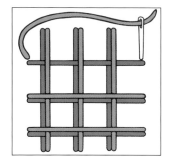 

1 Using the lightest or darkest colour, work a series of vertical straight stitches spaced evenly apart. Using the same colour, work a series of horizontal stitches, positioned to the bottom left of the design area, as shown.

2 Change to the next lightest or darkest colour. Work the same stitches with this thread, positioning them to the right of the vertical stitches already laid and just above the horizontal ones. Keep the stitches parallel and touching the previous set.

3 Repeat twice more, using the next two colours in order. Tie down the last set of stitches where they cross by working a small diagonal stitch from right to left in a matching or contrasting colour.

Brick and Cross Filling

Brick and cross
filling is one of many
decorative filling
stitches in crewel
embroidery that looks
more complicated than
it is.

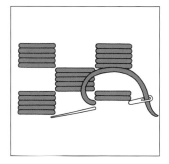 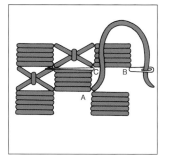 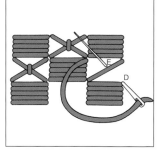

1 Work blocks of five horizontal satin stitches (see page 100) in a chequered sequence. The spacesbetween blocks should be the same size as the blocks themselves.

2 Using the same or a different colour, work a cross in each space between the blocks. To do this, bring the needle out at A and insert it at B, bringing it back out at C.

3 Insert the needle at D and bring it out in the centre of the space at E.

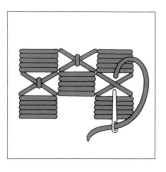

4 Make a tiny tying stitch over the cross to complete it.

Brick Satin Filling

Brick satin filling is satin stitch (see page 100) worked in a castellated arrangement. This can be worked in tones of one colour to create a shaded effect and add interest to large areas of stitching.

1 Work the first row in the first colour, starting at A. Work four long satin stitches, following the outer design line, then work four short stitches, just under half the length of the previous stitches. Repeat to the end.

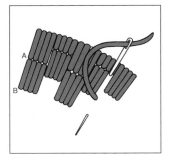

2 On the next row work repeated blocks of four long stitches, starting at B, to maintain the castellated pattern.

3 Continue in this way until the whole shape is filled. On the final row (C) you will need to adjust the size of the stitches to fit the space, as shown.

Burden Stitch

Burden stitch is a form of couching in which the tying stitches are longer than necessary for a decorative effect. It can be worked in two toning colours – one for the horizontal stitches and another for the verticals – to give further definition.

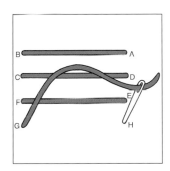

1 Work a series of horizontal straight stitches across the area to be filled, keeping them evenly spaced and working in the order A–B, C–D, E–F, G–H, and so on.

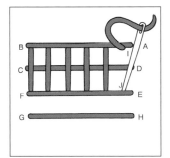

2 Change to the second colour, if desired. Work vertical stitches, from I–J, between A–B and E–F, taking stitches over C–D, as shown.

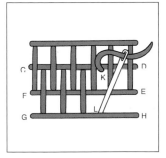

3 Work vertical stitches, from K–L, between C–D and G–H, taking stitches over E–F, as shown.

4 Continue in the same way until the whole area has been filled. On the final line you will need to work shorter stitches, from M–N, to fit the design area.

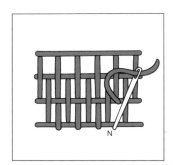

Buttonhole Block Shading

Buttonhole block shading creates textured bands that work well in rows to fill a large area. You can work the rows in shades of one colour for added interest. Worked in a single row (see page 29), buttonhole stitch is used in the Sleeping Mask (see page 94) and Flora Bolster (see page 104).

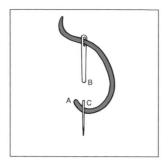

1 Bring the needle out at A and insert it at B, bringing it back out at C with the thread under the needle. A and C should be in a straight line on the lower edge of the area to be filled.

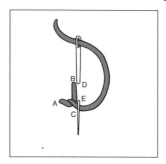

2 Make a second buttonhole stitch next to the first one by inserting the needle at D and bringing it out at E with the thread under the needle. Continue to the end of the line.

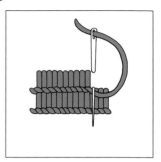

3 Work a second row of buttonhole stitch immediately above the first, in a slightly lighter or darker shade if you wish. Angle the stitches slightly as necessary to fit curved shapes. Work further rows as required to fill the area.

Buttonhole Scale Filling

Buttonhole scale filling is, as its name suggests, rather like fish scales in effect. The scales can be worked to varying depths and widths to fill a space and you can use different tones to create a variegated or shaded effect.

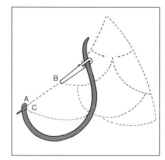

1 Bring the needle out at A and insert it at B, bringing it back out at C with the thread under the needle to make the first buttonhole stitch.

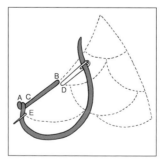

2 Insert the needle at D, beside B, and bring it back out at E with the thread under the needle. Continue in the same way, working the stitches close together, as shown.

3 Follow the scales of the design, working the knots of one scale over the ends of the stitches of the previous row.

Buttonhole Square Filling

Buttonhole square filling is a regular arrangement of blocks of buttonhole stitches to form a chequered pattern. The number of stitches in the blocks can be varied and small single stitches, such as French knots (see page 96), can be worked in the gaps to vary the effect still further.

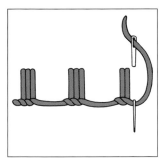

1 Work buttonhole stitches in groups of the required number of stitches – here there are three. The groups should be equally spaced.

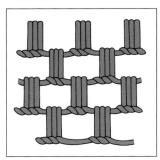

2 For the second row, work the same size groups of buttonhole stitches across the gaps of the previous row, as shown.

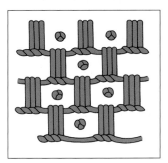

3 If desired place a stitch in the centre of the spaces. Here a French knot is used.

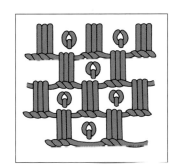

4 A detached chain stitch (see page 90) is a good alternative to fill the gaps.

Buttonhole Triangle Filling

Buttonhole triangle filling is an open filling that is useful for creating a lacy effect. Working different triangles in different tones lends it a patchwork feel.

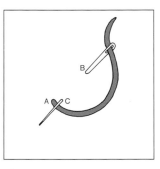

1 Bring the needle out at A and insert it at B, above right, bringing it back out at C to make a sloping buttonhole stitch.

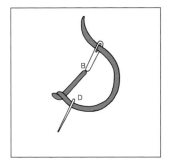

2 Insert the needle at B again and bring it out at D, a short distance from C, to work the next stitch.

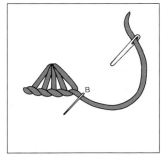

3 Work five buttonhole stitches, all meeting at B, spacing the knots on the lower edge to form a triangle.

4 Work further groups of triangles, as shown, building up the pattern to fill the design space.

Up and Down Buttonhole Stitch

Up and down buttonhole stitch has a smooth, neat finish and the double thread of each 'leg' gives it good definition. It is used in the Sleeping Mask (see page 94).

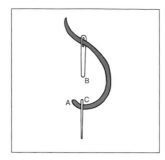

1 Bring the needle out at A and insert it at B, bringing it back out at C, close by A, with the thread under the needle.

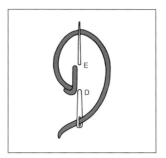

2 Pull the thread through. Insert the needle at D, close to C and take a stitch straight upward, coming out at E, next to B, and keeping the thread under the needle, as shown.

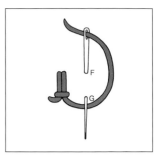

3 Pull through gently, first in an upwards movement then downwards to tighten the stitch. Leave a gap and then insert the needle at F, bringing it out at G. Repeat steps 2 and 3 to the end of the row.

Chain Stitch

Chain stitch is a popular open outline stitch that is one of the first stitches many people learn. When a single stitch is worked it is known as a detached chain stitch. Chain stitch is used in both the Sleeping Mask (see page 94) and Flora Bolster (see page 104).

1 Bring the needle out at A, hold the thread down and insert the needle back through the same hole.

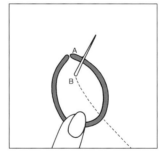

2 Bring the needle out at B and, keeping the thread under the needle, pull it gently to form a loop.

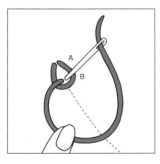

3 Insert the needle back through the hole at B. Bring the needle out a stitch length along the design line and repeat step 2 to make the next loop in the chain.

4 Finish the final loop with a small tying stitch, as shown. A single loop held down with a tying stitch is called detached chain stitch.

Chain Stitch Filling

Chain stitch filling is made by working close rows of chain stitch. The effect can be adjusted by working large stitches for an open effect or small stitches for a dense texture. Working concentric rings in different tones of a colour produces a three-dimensional visual effect.

1 Work a line of chain stitches around the edge of the area to be filled, as explained opposite, below.

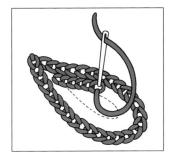

2 Work the next and subsequent rows inside the previous row, leaving no space between rows.

Chessboard Filling

Chessboard filling is a traditional crewel embroidery stitch that you will see in antique embroideries. Satin stitch blocks are worked in a chequered pattern, as for brick and cross filling (see page 86), but the stitched blocks have a cross worked on top of them, which can be in a contrast colour.

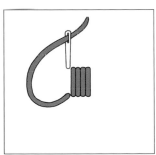

1 Work sets of five satin stitches (see page 100) to form blocks in a chequered pattern. The spaces between blocks should be the same size as the blocks themselves.

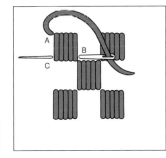

2 When you have completed the final block, bring the thread through at A, top left, and insert the needle at B, bottom right, bringing it back out at C, bottom left.

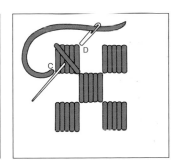

3 Insert the needle at D, top right of the block and bring it out midway along the diagonal stitch, passing the needle under that stitch.

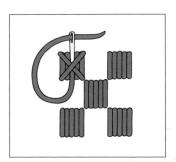

4 Take the needle over the cross that has now been formed and insert it just above to secure the cross. Repeat on the remaining satin stitch blocks.

Cloud Filling

Cloud filling is an attractive weaving stitch, and although it may look as if the short vertical stitches are tying stitches, these are actually worked first and the long stitches woven between them. Use one colour for the vertical stitches and a second colour for the weaving thread.

1 Stitch a line of small, evenly-spaced vertical stitches across the area to be filled. Work another line underneath, spacing these stitches between those of the first row. Repeat this pattern to fill the area.

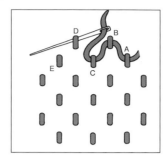

2 Change to a tapestry needle and a new colour of thread. Weave this thread between the stitches of the first and second rows, as shown, working from right to left.

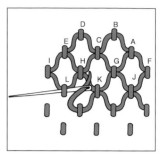

3 When you finish the first line, start the next, this time working between the second and third rows of straight stitches and again working from right to left. Continue in the order shown.

Coral Stitch

Coral stitch is a knot stitch that is often used for outlines or to suggest stems and twigs, but it is also an effective filling stitch when contrasting texture is required. To use it as a filling stitch, work it in close rows.

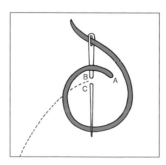

1 Bring the needle out at A, insert it at B and bring it back out at C, wrapping the thread over and under the needle, as shown.

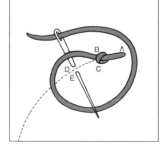

2 Pull through gently to draw up the knot. Repeat, inserting the needle at D and bringing it out at E to work the next knot. Repeat at regular intervals.

3 To work this stitch as a filling, stagger the position of the knots on adjacent lines, as shown.

Fly Stitch

Fly stitch is a versatile stitch that can be used singly, as a scattered filling, in rows as a border, or as a close filling. The tying stitch that secures the loop can be short, so that the stitch resembles a V, or long so that it resembles a Y.

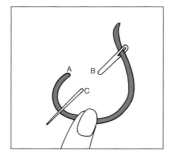

1 Bring the needle out at A, hold the thread down and insert the needle a little to the right at B (level with A). Bring the needle back out at C, below and halfway between A and B.

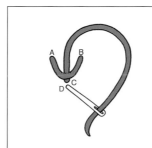

2 Keeping the thread under the needle, pull the thread through. Insert the needle at D to make a small tying stitch in the centre.

descriptive stitches

Some stitches are very obviously useful for describing a particular element in a representational embroidery: fly stitches make wonderful birds flying in the sky. The plant-like stitches, such as fern stitch (see page 37) and leaf stitch (see page 39) are other obvious choices. However, do use these stitches with care in this way or your embroidery can look a bit stale.

Four-Legged Knots

Four-legged knots are small, upright knots that can be used as a single stitch or grouped for a filling or textural peppering – in the same way as French knots (see page 96). The arms of each cross should be of equal length.

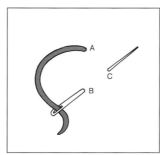

1 Bring the needle out at A and insert it directly below at B. Bring the needle back out at C, halfway between A and B and to the right.

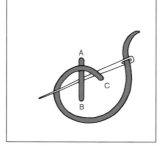

2 Without piercing the fabric, pass the needle between A and C and under the stitch A–B, then wrap the thread under the needle, as shown above. Pull the thread gently to tighten the knot.

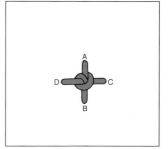

3 Insert the needle at D to complete the knot.

Sleeping mask

Add a little film star glamour to bedtime with this embroidered sleep mask. The stitches are simple to work and the mask is easy to make up once the embroidery is complete. Though this would make a wonderful gift for a girlfriend, you may find it hard to give away.

MATERIALS

- Piece of sateen cotton measuring 25 x 25cm (10 x 10in) and piece measuring 22 x 15cm (8¾ x 6 in)
- Mask template (see page 170)
- Paper scissors
- Fading fabric marker
- Transfer equipment
- 20cm (8in) ring frame
- Anchor Stranded Cotton: one skein in each of colours 232, 233, 400, 403, 851,1064,1066 and a colour to match the ribbon
- Size 10 embroidery needle
- Fabric scissors
- Pins
- Two lengths of 1.5-cm (⅝-in) wide ribbon, each measuring 40cm (16in)
- Sewing machine
- Sewing thread to match fabric colour

STITCHES USED

- Buttonhole stitch (see page 29)
- Up and down buttonhole stitch (see page 90)
- Chain stitch (see page 90)
- French knots (see page 96)
- Stem stitch (see page 101)

THE EMBROIDERY

Enlarge the template by 200 per cent and cut it out around the outer line (the inner dotted line is the stitching line and is shown only to help you position the eyes). Place the template centrally on the larger piece of fabric and draw around it with the fading fabric marker. Using the dressmaker's carbon paper or prick and pounce technique (see pages 16 and 17), transfer the eyes onto the outlined mask. Fix the fabric into the ring frame (see page 18).

Embroider the eyes using two strands of Stranded Cotton unless otherwise stated. For the open eye, embroider the top curve in chain stitch in colour 233. Embroider the eyelashes in stem stitch in colour 403. Embroider the bottom eyelashes in up and down buttonhole stitch using one strand of colour 403. The iris is close rows of stem stitch; outer two rows are colour 1064, the middle two are colour 1066 and the inner two are colour 851. The highlights are French knots in colour 232.

For the closed eye, embroider the curve in chain stitch in colour 400. Embroider the eyelashes in stem stitch in colour 403.

MAKING UP

Take the fabric out of the frame and cut out the embroidered mask. Pin a length of ribbon to each side, level with the eyes. The end of the ribbon must align with the edge of the mask and the rest of it lie across the mask. Roll each ribbon up and pin it to the mask to keep it out of the way of the stitching to come.

Cut another mask out of the smaller piece of fabric. Lay it right side down on top of the embroidered mask and pin, then tack the layers together, trapping the ends of the ribbon in the stitching.

Set the sewing machine to a small straight stitch. Taking a 1cm (⅜in) seam allowance and starting above one eye, sew around the mask, leaving a 5cm (2in) gap for turning through.

Turn the mask through, being careful not to prick yourself on the pins. Take the pins out and finger-press the seam all around. Press the seam with the iron, pressing under the seam allowance across the gap. Slip stitch the gap closed. Trim the ends of the ribbon at an angle.

Using one strand of pink thread, work buttonhole stitch around the edge of the mask, closing the gap as you stitch.

getting it right

Choose a dark, fine-woven fabric to block out as much light as possible. If you want a thicker mask, interline it with a layer of domette. To do this, cut out the mask shape in domette and trim it down to the stitching line. Once you have sewn the front and back of the mask together, tack the domette to the line of machine stitching before turning the mask right side out.

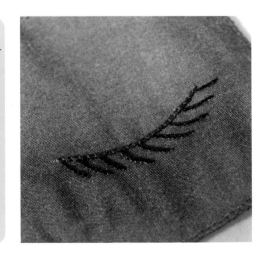

French Knots

French knots can be used singly or grouped for a filling. When used as a filling the knots can be tightly packed or randomly spaced, or both in a single area to give a three-dimensional look. These knots are used in both the Sleeping Mask (see page 94) and the Flora Bolster (see page 104).

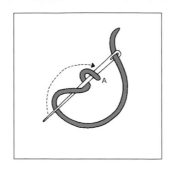

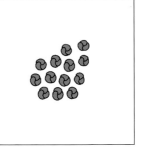

1 Bring the needle out at A, where the knot will be, and wrap the thread once or twice around it.

2 Holding the thread firmly, twist the needle back around and insert it very close to A.

3 Holding the wraps down on the front, pull the thread through and tighten the knot. If you are working a single knot, secure the thread with a tiny stitch underneath the knot. If it's a group of knots, just move on to the next one.

French Knots on Stalks

French knots on stalks are simply French knots with long tails. These are extremely useful for rendering flower buds or stamens. See them in the Flora Bolster (see page 104).

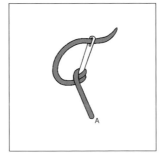

1 Bring the needle out at A, at the bottom of the stalk, and wrap the thread twice around it.

2 Turn the needle and insert it into the fabric at the place where the knot is to be positioned.

3 Pull the needle through to tighten the knot. To form a group of buds or stamens, bring the needle through at A again, ready to work the second French knot on a stalk.

Closed Herringbone Stitch

Closed herringbone is like a line of cross stitches, but with the stitches overlapping. The crosses can be off-centre, so they have longer 'legs' than 'arms'. The open version is the same, except that the stitches are placed further apart, though still overlapping (see page 39).

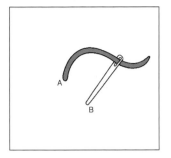

1 Bring the needle out at A and insert it diagonally down to the right at B.

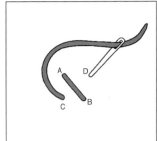

2 Bring the needle out at C and insert it at D to complete the cross.

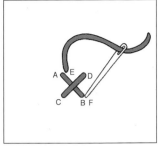

3 Bring the needle out at E, immediately beside A, and work a second cross parallel to the first one.

4 Continue in this way to the end of the row. If this stitch is being used to fill a curved area, keep the crossing points of all the stitches aligned.

Honeycomb Filling

Honeycomb filling is a weaving stitch that is worked in three related colours. It is created by laying straight stitches across the fabric, then a layer at 45 degrees and finally weaving at right angles to the second layer to create a mesh effect.

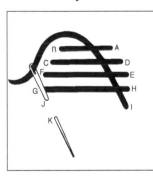

1 Using the first colour, work lines of equally spaced horizontal stitches across the design area in the order shown.

2 In the second colour work diagonal straight stitches across the area, maintaining the same spacing as before.

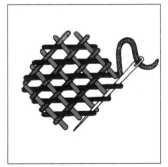

3 Change to the third colour. Working on the opposite diagonal, carefully weave the needle through the previous stitches, taking it over the diagonal stitches and under the horizontal ones.

Laid Work

Laid work is a term used to describe laying threads over the fabric and catching them down, often with a contrast colour thread. It is a quick way of working and creates a dense coverage that is useful for filling quite large areas decoratively.

1 Using the first colour, fill the design area with satin stitch (see page 100).

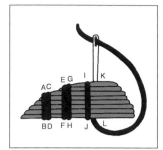

2 With a contrast thread, bring the needle out at A and insert it at B on the lower edge of the design area. Work a parallel stitch C–D. Leave a gap and work another pair of stitches, then repeat pairs of stitches at evenly-spaced intervals.

3 Work small horizontal tying stitches across the vertical threads, as shown. Keep these stitches regularly spaced and even across the area. Use the same colour or a contrast colour thread.

Long and Short Stitch

Long and short stitch is an essential part of crewelwork and is quite often the main stitch used to work a design. Working the rows in different shades of a colour can create excellent shading effects. This stitch is used in the Flora Bolster (see page 104).

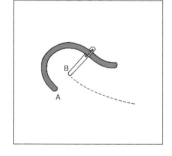

1 Bring the needle out at A and insert it at B, on the edge of the design area.

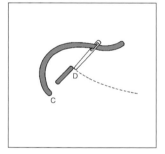

2 Bring the needle out at C and insert it at D, making a longer stitch that butts up tightly against the first stitch.

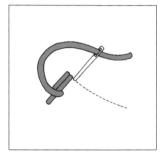

3 Repeat these two stitches to the end of the row.

4 On subsequent rows, bring the needle up through the stitch in the previous row. Work stitches that are the same length, but stagger the starting points, as shown.

Plate Stitch

Plate stitch produces a close texture that looks rather like rows of satin stitch (see page 100), but with strong divisions between the rows. It is worked in two rows at a time and you can change the colour of the thread between each pair of rows to create a graduated effect.

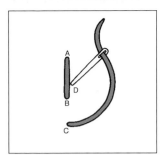

1 Bring the needle out at A and insert it at B, a short distance below. Bring the needle through at C, below A and a little to the right, and insert it again at D, a little higher than A.

2 Repeat the sequence along the row.

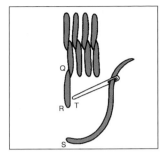

3 Work subsequent rows of stitches directly beneath, as shown.

Romanian Stitch

Romanian stitch is also known as Romanian couching, though you are only using one thread. It looks quite like Cretan stitch (see page 36) and is a simpler alternative. Stitches can be worked to varying lengths to fill a shape.

1 Bring the needle out at A, insert it at B and bring it back out at C.

2 Insert the needle at D on the opposite design line and bring it out at E, as shown, keeping the thread under the needle.

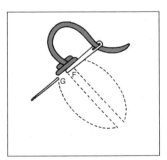

3 Insert the needle at F and bring it out at G, this time with the thread above the needle. Repeat steps 2 and 3 to fill the shape.

Satin Stitch

Satin stitch is a popular filling stitch. It looks simple but it takes a bit of practice to get the stitches to lie smoothly on the fabric with the edges even. This stitch is used in the Flora Bolster (see page 104).

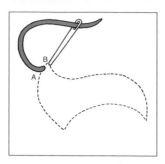

1 Bring the needle out at A and insert it at B on the opposite side of the shape to be filled, working on the design lines.

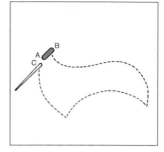

2 Bring the needle out at C, close to A.

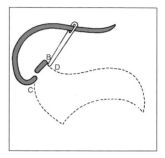

3 Insert the needle at D, close to B. Continue in the same way, placing the stitches very close together so that no background fabric shows. Keep the edges of the shape even and neat.

Satin Fan

Satin fan is simply an arrangement of satin stitches (see above) in a fan shape. Rows can be worked in graded tones of a single colour for a shaded effect.

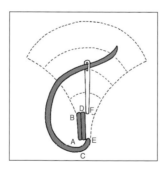

1 Bring the needle out at A and work a row of satin stitches of equal length at the base of the fan shape. Angle the stitches slightly as necessary.

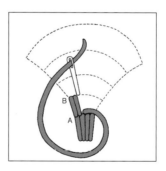

2 Changing to a deeper shade, if required, work a second line of satin stitches above the first, again keeping the stitches even.

3 Work each row of satin stitches in the same way, working to the shape of the fan.

Seeding

Seeding is a random arrangement of short straight stitches that is excellent for filling medium-sized areas quickly, as in the Flora Bolster (see page 104).

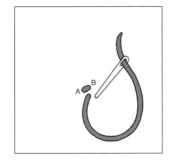

1 Bring the needle out at A and make a small straight stitch, inserting the needle at B. Then bring the needle out a short distance away and make another stitch of the same length at a different angle. Continue in this way to fill the design area.

Split Stitch

Split stitch is a delicate outline stitch that looks a little like fine chain stitch. It is also useful for outlining a specific area of a design before it is filled with other stitches. It is used in the Flora Bolster (see page 104).

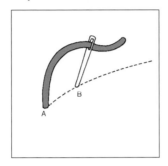

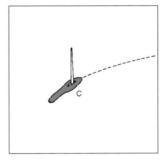

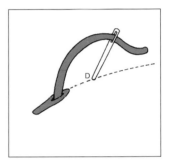

1 Bring the needle out at A and insert it at B.

2 Bring the needle out at C, piercing the thread of the previous stitch.

3 Insert the needle at D to form the next stitch. Continue in this way, following the design line.

Stem Stitch

Stem stitch is a popular outline stitch that can also be used as a filling when several rows are worked next to each other. It is a common component of crewelwork designs and is used in both the Sleeping Mask (see page 94), and the Flora Bolster (see page 104).

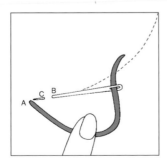

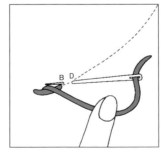

1 Bring the needle out at the start of the design line at A. Insert it at B and bring it out at C, midway between A and B, holding the thread to the right, as shown.

2 Pull the thread through. Hold the thread to the right and insert the needle at D, bringing it out at B. Continue, making the stitches the same length.

3 When working stem stitch as a filling, work the lines close together for a rope-like effect. If the thread is held to the left, the stitch is called outline stitch.

Portuguese Knotted Stem Stitch

Portuguese knotted stem stitch is a variation of stem stitch (see page 101) with a pronounced knot in it for a thicker, bolder line. A similar-looking alternative is coral stitch (see page 92). This stitch is used in the Flora Bolster (see page 104).

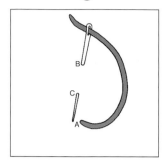

1 Bring the needle out at A and insert it immediately above at B, making a vertical stitch. Bring the needle back out at C, midway between A and B.

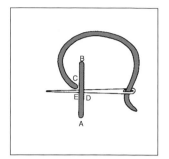

2 Make a tying stitch around A–B, going over A–B and back under to E, near to C, without piercing the fabric.

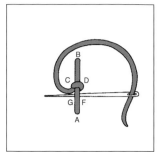

3 Make a second tying stitch below the first one, from F to G, as shown.

4 Begin the next stitch by inserting the needle at H and bringing it back out at B. The distance between H and B should be half the distance from A to B. Continue to the end of the line.

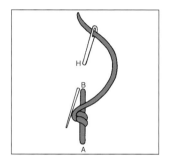

Tête de Boeuf

Tête de boeuf is French for 'bull's head' and you can see why. This stitch can be used as the base of a flower, massed as a filling, used as a seeding stitch or in rows as a border.

1 Bring the needle out at A and make a short diagonal stitch to B to make one horn of the bull's head.

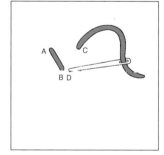

2 Bring the needle out at C, level with A, and make a short diagonal stitch to D for the other horn.

3 Bring the needle out at E, between the two diagonal stitches. Holding a loop of thread below the stitch, insert the needle beside E and bring it out at F, a short distance below, to make a chain stitch (see page 90).

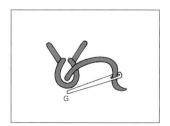

4 Tighten the stitch gently and insert the needle at G to complete the stitch.

Trellis Square Filling

Trellis square filling, also known as Jacobean couching, creates a decorative effect over a trellis of straight stitches. The decorations can be applied in a variety of ways to create different effects. This filling is typical of traditional crewelwork.

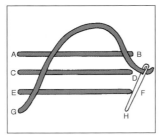

1 Lay rows of evenly-spaced horizontal stitches over the area to be covered. They should lie smoothly against the fabric without pulling.

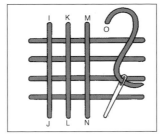

2 Work vertical stitches, spaced equally in the same way.

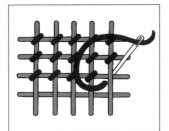

3 Using the same or a contrast colour thread, work small diagonal tying stitches over each intersection.

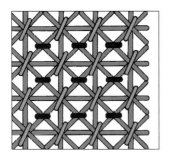

4 In this variation additional diagonal stitches were made in both directions. All the intersections are caught with either horizontal or diagonal tying stitches.

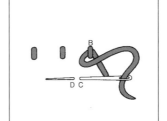

5 In this variation detached chain stitches (see page 90) and French knots (see page 96) add textural interest to the trellis.

Wave Stitch

Wave stitch is a weaving stitch that creates a honeycomb pattern that can be closed or lacy. The first row of stitches is woven into a series of small straight stitches, but subsequent rows are woven into the previous row.

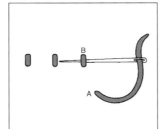

1 Work a row of small, evenly-spaced vertical stitches across the top of the design area. Bring the needle out at A and pass it through the first stitch at B without piercing the fabric.

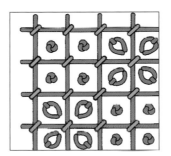

2 Make a small stitch from C to D. Repeat to weave the thread through all the straight stitches.

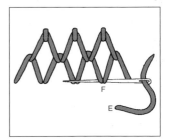

3 On the second and subsequent rows weave the thread behind the stitches of the previous row, as shown.

Flora bolster

Inspired by traditional crewel embroidery, but thoroughly updated in design and colours, this flora bolster is a stunning project. A good range of stitches is used to describe the motifs, though you can, of course, change them and use your own favourites if you prefer. Once the embroidery is done, the bolster is very quick and easy to make up: no special sewing skills are required. You can also use the design for a different project, such as a cushion or a table runner.

MATERIALS

- 80 x 80cm (31½ x 31½in) of herringbone weave cotton fabric in ecru
- Slate frame
- Tacking thread
- Hand-sewing needle
- Flora template (see page 171)
- Prick and pounce kit
- Watercolour paint
- Fine paintbrush
- Appletons Crewel Wool: one skein in each of colours 321, 322, 523, 525, 842, 844 and 864
- Size 5 embroidery needle
- Scissors
- Iron
- Pins
- Sewing thread to match fabric
- Sewing machine
- 45 x 17cm (18 x 6¾in) bolster pad
- Two 13cm (5in) circles of felt in mustard yellow
- Strong buttonhole thread to match fabric

STITCHES USED

- Buttonhole stitch (see page 29)
- Buttonhole scale filling (see page 88)
- Chain stitch (see page 90)
- French knots (see page 96)
- French knots on stalks (see page 96)
- Long and short stitch (see page 98)
- Satin stitch (see page 100)
- Seeding (see page 101)
- Split stitch (see page 101)
- Stem stitch (see page 101)
- Portuguese knotted stem stitch (see page 102)

THE EMBROIDERY

Fix the fabric into a slate frame (see page 19). Using tacking stitches, mark out a central 60 x 60cm (24 x 24in) square on the fabric (see page 16). Tack two more lines, one 8cm (3in) in from each side of the square; these mark the position of each end of the bolster pad. Enlarge the template by 200 per cent and, using the prick and pounce method (see page 17), transfer it onto the fabric, positioning it centrally in the tacked square. Carefully paint over the lines with watercolour paint and leave the paint to dry.

Referring to the stitch notes and wool colours on the template key, embroider the flora design.

MAKING UP

Take the embroidery out of the frame and cut it out around the edges of the outer tacked square. Press under 2cm (¾in) along each side edge. Open the pressed edges flat, pin the two raw edges right sides together and, taking a 1.5cm (⅝in) seam allowance, sew the seam to make a tube. Press the seam open and turn the tube right side out. Fold the pressed ends to the inside.

Pin a circle of mustard felt to each end of the bolster pad. Using oversewing stitches, sew the circles in place.

Slip the embroidered tube over the bolster pad, positioning the pad between the two remaining tacked lines. Using the buttonhole thread, work a line of gathering stitches around the pressed-under edge of one end of the bolster. Position the stitches close to the fold and make them about 1cm (⅜in) long. Pull the stitches up as tightly as possible and secure the thread with backstitches hidden in the troughs of the gathers. Repeat on the other end of the bolster. Take out the remaining tacking stitches.

getting it right

This is such a simple style of bolster to make. If it needs laundering, undo both the gathered ends and slip the pad out of the tube.

GOLDWORK

Gold has been prized throughout the world for centuries, so it's no surprise that embroideries worked in gold threads have been important for luxury items. However, modern production techniques have made goldwork threads affordable, and the colour and patina still give metal thread embroideries a rich, elegant feel.

The techniques require a different approach to all other forms of embroidery, but they are not difficult to learn and they lend themselves as well to contemporary designs as they do to medieval ones.

The Silver Brooch (see page 112) demonstrates perfectly how goldwork can be used to make a modern item, and it only requires two techniques. The pretty Acorns and Oak Leaves picture (see page 116) introduces a few more techniques, and the simplest ever framing method.

Stitching Goldwork

The metal threads used in goldwork are too thick and stiff to be sewn into fabric in the way threads are in other styles of embroidery; instead they are sewn onto the fabric using a variety of techniques. None of the methods are difficult to learn, but it's essential to work slowly and carefully for the best finish; even experienced embroiderers take their time with goldwork.

For general instructions for preparing fabric, transferring a design and starting and finishing stitching, turn to pages 14–22. Below is some further information that is specific to goldwork.

Fabrics

Goldwork is traditionally worked on either silk or velvet, though it is also effective on finely woven linen. Avoid loosely woven fabrics and patterned fabrics as the latter rarely look good. If you are using velvet, choose a cotton velvet rather than a silk or synthetic one as these tend to mark very easily. Whichever fabric you choose needs to be stabilised onto calico (see page 14) and framed up in a slate frame (see page 19).

Threads

Metal threads are commonly available in gold, silver and copper. Gold threads come in various qualities, from expensive 18 carat Japanese gold thread to gilt metallic thread, which is ideal if you are a goldwork novice. The threads will tarnish a little in time, but this can add a lovely vintage look to the embroidery. All metal threads are sewn to the fabric using a polyester sewing thread in a matching colour. For some techniques the sewing thread is drawn across beeswax to strengthen it before it is used.

There are various types of metal thread (see page 10): Japanese (or Jap) thread, also called passing thread, is a round thread made from a very thin strip of gold or foil twisted around a silk or cotton core. It comes in various weights and is couched onto the fabric.

Purl is made from super-fine wire tightly coiled, like a spring; though once stretched it will not recoil. Purls come in different textures and weights (the heavier weights are sometimes called bullion) and are either couched on, or cut into shorter lengths and sewn on by taking the needle and sewing thread through the coil. Pearl purl looks like a string of tiny beads (or pearls) and is very popular for outlines. Bright check purl has a triangular, rather than round, cross-section, making it catch the light and sparkle. The wire used to make smooth purl is so fine that the coils are almost invisible; this purl is tricky to use perfectly.

Twist is made up of two or more fine metal threads twisted together to form a cord; the number of plies affects the weight of the thread. This thread can be couched or sewn on invisibly with the needle going between the plies.

Rococo and check threads are made from a fine wire twisted around a cotton core. They are couched onto the background fabric.

Plate is flat metal strip, like ribbon, that is sewn onto the fabric with straight stitches across its width.

Equipment

Use a size 10, 11 or 12 embroidery needle (the finest you can manage) to sew on the metal threads, and a size 24 chenille needle for plunging (see page 110). A mellor (see page 13) is a specialist tool for helping position threads accurately and is invaluable (see Suppliers, page 174). Keep a pair of embroidery scissors just for goldwork, as cutting the metal threads will quickly blunt the blades. A cutting board made from a square of velvet glued to a piece of thick cardboard is a great surface for cutting short lengths of purl on (see page 13), as the pile of the velvet stops them springing about.

Starting to stitch

Goldwork is one of the only embroidery techniques in which it is fine to use a knot to start the sewing thread. The double layer fabric and heavy texture of the metal thread embroidery will stop knots showing on the surface. Finish off sewing threads by stitching into the back of an embroidered section.

Couching Metal Thread

Couching metal thread involves laying thread, such as Jap or passing, on the surface of the fabric and holding it in place with small stitches of sewing thread in a matching colour. Metal threads are usually couched in pairs. Couching is used in the Acorns and Oak Leaves picture (see page 116).

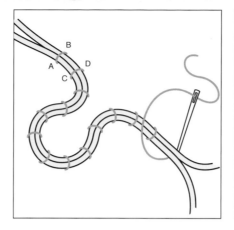

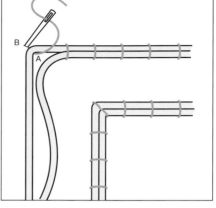

1 Leaving 5cm (2in) free, lay two strands of metal thread at the start of the design line. Thread a fine needle with sewing thread and knot one end. Bring the needle out at A and insert it at B, making a straight stitch at right angles to the metal threads. Then stitch from C to D. Couch along the threads, making straight stitches at 5mm (¼in) intervals and angling the stitches so that they are always at right angles to the metal threads.

2 To couch the metal threads around a right-angled or shallower corner, work with one thread at a time. Bring the needle and sewing thread out right on the corner, on the inside of the design line at A. Gently pull the outer metal thread around the sewing thread until it is lying at the desired angle. Make a diagonal stitch to B. Repeat the process with the second metal thread, butting it up closely to the first thread.

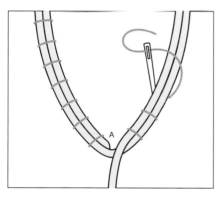

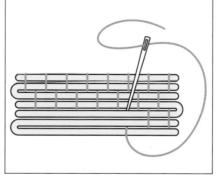

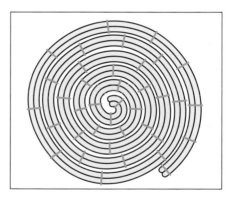

3 To couch metal threads around a point or a corner tighter than a right angle, bend and stitch the outer thread as before. Cut the inner thread 5cm (2in) beyond the last couching stitch and plunge it (see page 110) at A. Start the inner thread again on the other side of the corner, couching it together with the outer thread. When the design is complete, plunge the free end of the inner thread so that it dovetails with the end of the first thread.

4 When couching metal threads back and forth to fill an area, stitch them down in pairs, turning one thread and plunging the end of the other in the order shown. Stagger the couching stitches so they sit between those on the previous row; this is called 'bricking' the stitches.

5 A circle of couched threads is worked in a spiral from the centre out. To work the innermost circle, bring the needle out on the inside of the metal threads to make the couching stitches. On subsequent circles, lay the metal threads in position and bring the needle up on the outside of them and down on the inside, tight against the previous row of threads. Brick the couching stitches around the spiral.

Plunging

Plunging involves taking the ends of metal threads to the wrong side of the fabric to neaten them. Once on the wrong side, the ends of the threads are sewn to the back of the fabric with sewing thread.

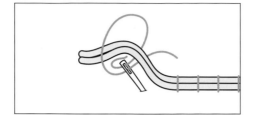

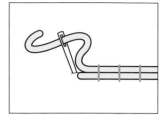

1 To plunge two ends together, use a lasso of strong sewing thread. Pass a short length of thread through the eye of a large tapestry needle and then pass it through again in the same direction to make a loop. Put the ends of the metal threads into the lasso. Insert the needle into the fabric where the threads need to disappear and slowly and carefully pull the lasso and ends of threads through to the back. Using a fine needle and sewing thread, firmly oversew the ends of thread to the back of the fabric. Make sure the stitches are on the back of an area covered by threads so that they do not show on the right side of the fabric.

2 To plunge just one end, thread it through the eye of a large tapestry needle. Pass the needle through the fabric, carefully pulling the end through. Sew the end in place, as before.

Couching Pearl Purl

Couching pearl purl is done in a slightly different way to metal threads. Pearl purl is couched in both the Silver Brooch (page 112) and the Acorns and Oak Leaves picture (see page 116).

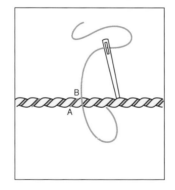

1 To couch pearl purl, first stretch it very gently to open up the coils just the tiniest amount (it is shown here slightly overstretched so you can see the stitching). Then cut it to length, as the ends of purl thread are not plunged. Thread a fine needle with sewing thread and knot one end. Lay the pearl purl on the design line. Bring the needle out at A and insert it at B, making a diagonal stitch in line with a coil of the pearl purl. Gently pull the sewing thread taut so that it slips between the coils and disappears. Make a stitch between each of the first two coils of the length, then make a stitch between every third coil. Finish with a stitch between each of the last two coils.

stretching pearl purl

First cut the pearl purl to slightly longer than is needed. Use your scissors (the ones kept especially for cutting gold threads; they will get blunt quite quickly) to grip one end of the length, slipping the blades between the first and second coils. Then pull very gently on the other end. The coils should not actually be separated, just have the tightness eased a little. However, creative goldwork pieces do use overstretched pearl purl sewn on with visible thread and the results can be gorgeous.

Cutwork

Cutwork can be used to cover an area with purl thread. The area to be covered must first be padded with felt or string (see page 115); in this sample felt has been used. Cutwork is used in the Acorns and Oak Leaves picture (see page 116).

1 Cut the purl to exactly the length required to cross the padding at an angle, as shown. Thread a fine needle with sewing thread and double it, knotting the ends together. Draw the thread across a block of beeswax to strengthen it. Bring the needle out on the edge of the padding at A. Thread on a cut length of purl and push it right down the thread. Insert the needle at B and pull the thread taut. Repeat to sew on further lengths of purl, butting them up closely so no felt shows.

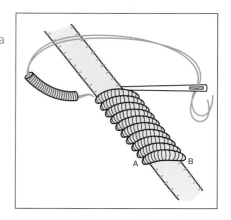

Purl Loops

Purl loops add a three-dimensional element to a goldwork embroidery. Keep them quite short and sew them on with doubled, beeswaxed thread, as used for cutwork (see above). Cut all the pieces of purl to length before you start.

1 Bring the needle out at A. Thread on a length of purl and insert the needle at B. The space between A and B must be wide enough to fit in both ends of the purl. Gently pull the thread through to form the loop.

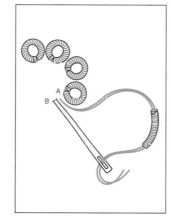

cutting to length

Once you have cut a first piece of purl to the right length, use it as a guide to cut a second piece exactly the same length. Keep this second piece to use as the guide to cut all subsequent pieces.

Chipping

Chipping is a quick and easy way to cover a larger area in a goldwork embroidery. The area to be covered must first be padded with felt (see page 115) and the chips are sewn on with doubled, beeswaxed thread, as used for cutwork (see above). Chipping is used in the Silver Brooch (see page 112) and the Acorns and Oak Leaves picture (see page 116).

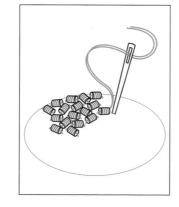

1 Cut tiny lengths of purl for the chips; each one should be only as long as it is wide. Bright check purl works very well for this technique as it is so sparkly. Bring the needle out, thread on a chip and slide it down the thread. Insert the needle at the other end of the chip. Pull the thread taut so the chip lies flat on the felt. Repeat the process, sewing on the chips at varying angles and fitting them tightly together so that no felt shows.

Silver brooch

This is a quick, easy-to-make accessory that will strike a quizzical note on a coat, hat, bag, or anything else you pin it to. Chipping always looks intricate, but it actually 'grows' quite quickly, so filling in this little shape won't take long.

MATERIALS

- Piece of grey felt measuring 15 x 15cm (6 x 6in)
- Question mark template (see page 170)
- 10cm (4in) ring frame
- Prick and pounce kit
- Watercolour paint
- Fine paintbrush
- Gilt pearl purl no. 1
- Silver-plated wire check no. 8
- Scissors for cutting gold thread
- Grey sewing thread
- Size 10 sharps needle
- Scissors
- Hand-sewing needle
- Brooch finding
- Fabric glue

STITCHES USED

- Couching pearl purl (see page 110)
- Chipping (see page 111)
- Buttonhole stitch (see page 29)

THE EMBROIDERY

Using the prick and pounce technique (see page 17), transfer the design onto the felt, positioning it centrally. Paint carefully over the lines and leave the paint to dry. Fix the felt into the ring frame (see page 18).

Use gilt pearl purl no. 1 to couch the outline of both parts of the question mark. Fill in the outlines with chipping in silver-plated wire check no. 8.

MAKING UP

Take the felt out of the ring frame. Very carefully, cut away excess around the edge of the embroidery leaving a narrow border.

From the felt, cut out a backing piece that is a bit larger than the question mark. Hand-sew the brooch finding to the back of this piece. Using just a bit of glue in the centre of the shape, stick the question mark to the backing, positioning it so that the brooch finding is towards the top of the question mark and centred left to right. When the glue is dry, cut out the backing around the edge of the question mark. Using grey sewing thread, buttonhole stitch the layers together around the edge.

getting it right

Working the patch on grey felt means that you don't have to pad the silver chipping (see page 111), so if you want the brooch border to be a different colour, you'll need some grey felt to pad the design with.

S-ing

S-ing is another method of stitching down purl threads. The pieces of thread are cut to length before starting and are sewn on with doubled, beeswaxed thread, as used for cutwork (see page 111).

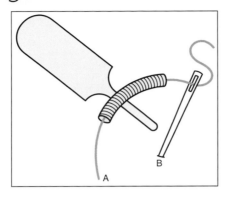

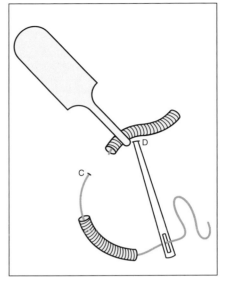

1 Bring the needle out at A on the design line and thread on a length of purl. Insert the needle at B and pull the thread taut. If need be, use a mellor to position the purl.

2 Bring the needle out at C, half a stitch length beyond A. Thread on a second length of purl. Hold the first purl to one side with the mellor and insert the needle at D, halfway between A and B.

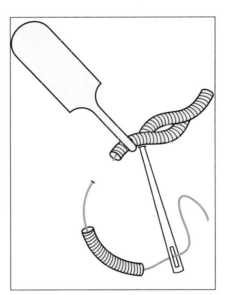

3 Repeat along the design line.

Twist

Twist is a metal thread made from two or more strands twisted together. It can be sewn down to create an outline, or in tightly packed rows to fill an area.

1 Thread a fine needle with sewing thread and draw it across beeswax for strength. Sew the twist down with tiny stitches sewn into the underside of it at the same angle as the strands are twisted together, as shown. The stitches should be invisible once pulled taut.

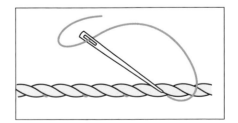

Plate

Plate is a flat metal ribbon that can be sewn down in a straight line, or it can be folded back and forth to fill an area with zigzags. These zigzags can be open, as here, or closed so that the background fabric does not show between them. The plate is held in place with a single length of matching sewing thread, drawn through beeswax for strength.

1 Bring the needle out at the edge of the shape to be filled at A. Take it across the plate (about 5mm (¼in) from the end), following the edge of the shape, and insert it at B. Fold the plate across over the stitch. Bring the needle out on the other side of the shape at C. Stitch across the plate to D, then fold the plate over on itself. Continue in this way, stitching the plate down on either side of the shape until it is filled.

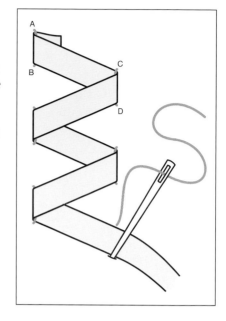

Basketwork

Basketwork is ideal for filling a large area with a woven texture. Any metal thread can be used, and you can alternate types of threads to achieve more visual texture.

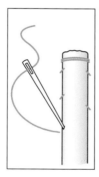

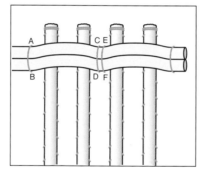

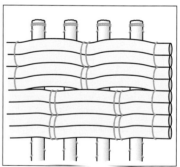

1 Lay evenly-spaced lengths of yellow string across the area to be covered. Using a fine needle and matching sewing thread, sew each length down with tiny straight stitches along each side and a double stitch across each end.

2 Using the couching method (see page 109) couch pairs of metal threads at right angles across the lengths of string. Leave 5cm (2in) free at each end to be plunged (see page 110) when the sewing is complete. Make one couching stitch from A to B before the first length of string, take the metal threads over the first and second lengths and make another stitch from C to D. Make a third stitch from E to F, before the third length of string and take the threads over the next two lengths of string. Repeat across the area, making a double stitch between each alternate length of string.

3 Couch a second pair of threads across the lengths of string, sewing them down in the same pattern as the first row. Then couch a third pair of threads in the same way, but sewing them down in between the strings skipped over in the first rows of couching to create the basket weave effect. Sew down a fourth pair of threads in the same pattern as the third pair. Repeat, sewing down double pairs of threads to cover the whole area.

Felt Padding

Felt padding involves covering the design area on a piece of fabric with yellow craft felt (grey felt if silver threads are being used) to create a raised surface, and to prevent the background fabric showing between stitched-down threads. Padding is used in the Acorns and Oak Leaves picture (see page 116).

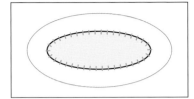

1 As many layers of padding can be used as needed; in this sample three layers are used. If you have used the prick and pounce technique (see page 17) to mark out the design, then use the pricked tracing paper as a template to cut the felt pieces from. If not, create a template of the design area from paper before cutting the felt. Cut the first layer of felt in the shape of the design area, but just one-third of the size. Position it in the design area and sew it down with sewing thread and tiny straight stitches. Bring the needle out just outside the edge of the felt and make a tiny stitch across the edge. Make stitches at the major compass points to tack the felt in place, then make further stitches about 5mm (¼in) apart all around the felt.

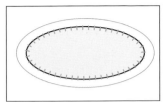

2 Cut the second layer of felt about two-thirds the size of the design area. Position it to cover the first layer and sew it down in the same way.

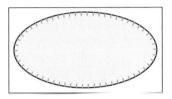

3 Cut the final layer to fit the design area exactly. Position it and sew it down as before, but make the stitches 2mm (⅛in) apart all around.

String Padding

String padding can be used to create higher, narrower shapes than those created by felt padding. Use soft yellow string (white string for silver threads), stitched down with matching sewing thread. Draw the string across beeswax before cutting it into the lengths required to fill the design area.

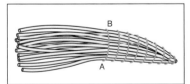

1 Group the lengths of string together into a firm bundle and position them in the middle of the design area. Bring the needle up at A and make a stitch over the bundle to B. Pull the thread taut, but not tight enough to make an indent in the bundle. Make more stitches across the bundle towards one end. (Here, the right-hand side is complete and we are working towards the left.)

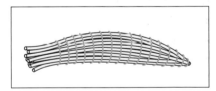

2 Carefully cut some threads away from the underside of the bundle so that the size of the bundle decreases, but the threads on the surface remain smooth.

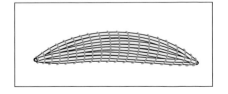

3 Continue making stitches across the bundle and trimming threads away from the underside so that the bundle of string fits neatly into the design area. Finish the bundle with a stitch into the end of the remaining pieces of string.

Acorns and oak leaves

Much embroidery is framed and hung as artwork, and looks beautiful treated in this way. However, traditional framing can be both expensive and old-fashioned, so consider extending a sewing theme by framing your work in an embroidery hoop. The result is fresh and pretty and looks at home in any interior. This embroidery uses a wide range of goldwork techniques, but as it is small it will not take too long to work.

MATERIALS

- Piece of silk fabric measuring 20 x 20cm (8 x 8in)
- Acorns and oak leaf template (see page 170)
- Piece of calico measuring 20 x 20cm (8 x 8in)
- 15cm (6in) ring frame
- Prick and pounce kit
- Watercolour paint
- Fine paintbrush
- Yellow craft felt
- Gilt pearl purl no. 1
- Gilt smooth passing no. 4
- Art gold bright check no. 6
- Silver-plated wire check no. 8
- Silver-plated smooth purl no. 8
- Scissors for cutting gold thread
- Grey and yellow sewing threads
- Size 10 sharps needle
- 10cm (4 in) ring frame
- Fabric scissors
- Piece of felt measuring 11 x 11cm (4½ x 4½in)
- Pencil
- Sewing thread to match the felt colour
- Curved quilting needle (optional)
- 20cm (8in) of narrow satin ribbon

STITCHES USED

- Buttonhole stitch (see page 29)
- Chipping (see page 111)
- Couching metal thread (see page 109)
- Couching pearl purl (see page 110)
- Cutwork (see page 111)

THE EMBROIDERY

Using the prick and pounce technique (see page 17), transfer the design onto the silk fabric, positioning it centrally. Paint carefully over the lines and leave the paint to dry. Lay the silk over the calico and, treating the two layers as one, fix the fabric into the 15cm (6in) ring frame (see page 18). Stabilise the silk onto the calico (see page 14).

Pad the caps of the acorns with a single layer of craft felt (see page 115).

Use gilt pearl purl no. 1 to couch the outline of the leaves and the stem of the acorns. Couch a double line of gilt smooth passing no. 4 around the inside of the pearl purl leaf outline and tight against it, taking the thread right down the stem to fill it. Use couched gilt pearl purl no. 1 for the central leaf veins and cutwork in silver-plated smooth purl no. 8 for the smaller veins.

Outline the outer edges of the acorn caps with gilt pearl purl no. 1 and fill each cap with chipping in art gold bright check no. 6. Fill the lower half of each acorn with cutwork in silver-plated wire check no. 8.

MAKING UP

Take the fabric out of the ring frame. Very carefully, cut away excess calico fabric around the edge of the embroidery.

Lay the inner hoop of the 10cm (4in) ring frame on the felt and draw around the outside of it. Cut out the circle, cutting just inside the drawn line.

Fix the embroidered silk into the small frame, positioning the design centrally and making sure the screw is at the top. Fasten the screw very tightly. Cut the fabric in a circle about 4cm (1¾in) outside the frame. Finger-press a 1cm (⅜in) hem all around. Using doubled thread, work a line of running stitch around the edge of the circle, close to the folded edge. Pull the gathers up tightly and secure the thread. Lace across the gathers in a similar way to lacing across the back of a mounted embroidery (see page 21) to make them as tight and flat as possible.

Lay the felt circle on the back of the gathers and pin it in place around the edge. Using matching thread, buttonhole stitch the felt to the fabric all around the edge: you may find it easiest to use a curved quilting needle to do this.

PULLED THREAD

Pulled thread is a form of counted thread embroidery with a difference. The embroidery thread is pulled so tightly that the strands of the fabric are distorted and a decorative pattern of holes is made.

The origins of pulled thread embroidery can be traced back to ancient Egypt, though in Europe it was most popular in the 18th century when it was often designed to mimic expensive lace and was worked on fabric with up to 100 strands per inch. However, gorgeous designs can be worked on a more manageable 28 strands per inch evenweave fabric. The simpler of the two projects, the Diamond Bracelet (see page 128) offers a fresh interpretation of traditional pulled thread, while coloured threads are used to quirky effect in the Cupcake Apron (see page 136).

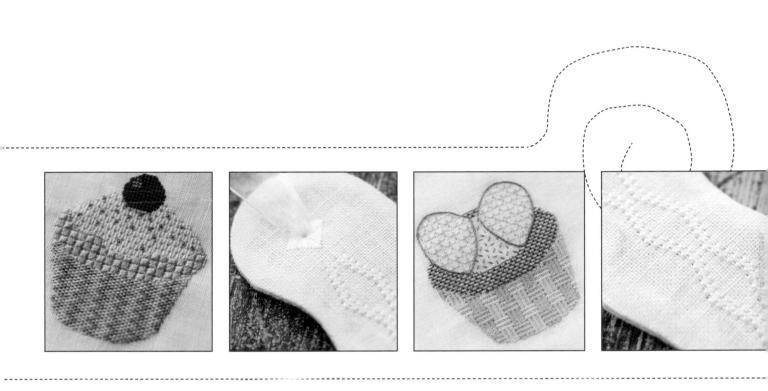

Stitching Pulled Thread

Pulled thread requires various techniques not used in other forms of embroidery, so it's important to read this section carefully if you are new to this technique. For general instructions for preparing fabric, transferring a design, and starting and finishing stitching, turn to pages 14–22.

Fabrics

Look for an evenweave fabric (see page 8 for more details) that is not too tightly woven or you won't be able to pull the fabric into the required design. If necessary, push a tapestry needle between the threads on a corner of the fabric and see if the threads move apart quite easily. Linen is the traditional favourite for all counted thread work and many embroiderers feel that the needle slides between the threads more smoothly than with any other fabric. It is available in many weights and thread counts from 14 to 32 strands to the inch.

Cotton is also traditional and comes in counts of up to 28 strands to the inch, which is suitable for all but the very finest of pulled thread work. Hardanger fabric (see page 8 for more details) in a fine count, such as 22 strands to the inch, can be used for pulled thread work, but the lower counts have a tendency to look very chunky and naïve.

Threads

Thread must be strong because you have to pull quite hard on it; there is nothing worse than a thread snapping in the middle of a long row of stitching. Traditionally it should also be the same thickness as the fabric threads and the best way of checking this is to pull off a strand from the edge of the fabric and lay it next to the proposed sewing thread; they should be roughly the same thickness. The projects in this chapter are worked in two strands of Anchor Stranded Cotton (see page 10 for more details).

Another popular thread is Anchor Pearl Cotton no. 12, the finest in the range. This is strong enough to withstand the tension of the most firmly pulled stitches and comes in a range of colours. Anchor Coton à Broder comes in various thicknesses (called 'tickets') and ticket no. 16 is the most popular thickness and is also available in a range of colours.

Needle

Use a tapestry needle when working pulled thread, so that you push between the fabric threads rather than piercing them. A size 24 or 26 tapestry needle will usually be suitable.

Charts

Like all counted thread work, pulled thread is stitched from a chart. The grid lines of the charts represent the strands of the fabric. The charts show the stitch patterns with the thread relaxed, not pulled tight, so that you can clearly see how the stitches are made. The effect once the threads are pulled tight can be very different, so it is worth trying a stitch on a scrap of project fabric before you start a piece.

If you are filling a complex shape with a stitch pattern, you will probably need to work partial stitches to fill the edges of the area. Work all the complete pattern stitches first, then work the partial stitches as best you can to give the look of the pattern continuing beyond the design area.

Starting to stitch

The darning method (see page 22) is the best way to start the thread once the pattern is underway, though initially you'll need to use either the waste knot or the in-line method (see page 22). Finish a thread by weaving it into the back of stitches.

Pulling the thread

How tight you pull the thread depends both on the stitch being used and the effect you want. It's always best to experiment with a stitch on a scrap of the project fabric to decide on the tension before you start. Always work a particular stitch with the same tension throughout to avoid it looking untidy. The stitches on pages 134–135 are complementary to the patterns and should not be pulled tight. If you are starting with the darning technique, you can usually pull the first stitch tight. If not, you can start with an un-pulled stitch or, if the thread and fabric match, make a tiny securing backstitch before the start of the stitch pattern. A backstitch can also be used if need be to secure a line of pulled threads before turning a corner in a pattern. Alternatively, make a securing knot through the back of a previous stitch before turning the corner.

Algerian Filling Stitch

Algerian filling stitch is simply satin stitch (see page 135) worked in stepped blocks. Each block is made up of three stitches worked over four strands. Work in horizontal rows, stitching alternate blocks, as shown, and pulling the stitches firmly.

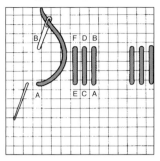

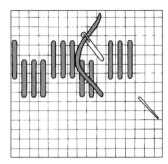

1 Bring the needle out at A and insert it four fabric strands above at B. Bring the needle out at C and insert it at D, out at E and insert it at F to complete the group of three stitches. Begin the next group four strands to the left and continue in the same way to the end of the row.

2 Work the next row from left to right, stepping the blocks down two strands and placing them between the blocks of the previous row, as shown. Repeat these two rows to fill the design area.

Backstitch Rings

Backstitch rings is backstitch worked in an octagonal ring. It is worked from right to left as a series of half rings, which are completed by working back across the row. All stitches must be pulled firmly.

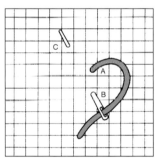

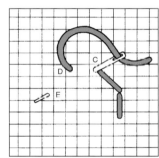

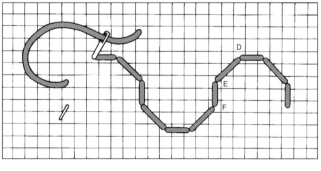

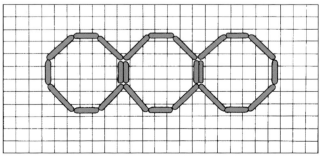

1 Bring the needle out at A, insert it at B, two fabric strands down, and bring it out at C.

2 Insert the needle at A and bring it out at D, in at C and out at E.

3 The stitch F to E both completes the first half ring and starts the second one. Then work a half ring pointing downwards, then another one facing upwards, and so on.

4 Turn the fabric around and work back across the row in mirror image to complete the rings.

Chequer Filling Stitch

Chequer filling stitch creates a pretty, starry design. It is worked diagonally first one way and then the other, with the stitches pulled firmly. It can be worked as single rows or to cover large areas with an all-over pattern.

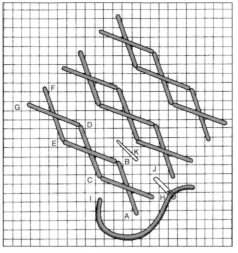

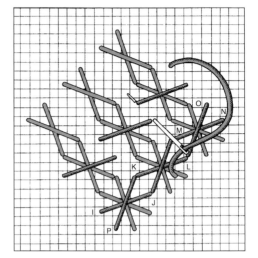

1 Bring the needle out at A and insert it at B, six fabric strands up and two strands to the left. Bring the needle out at C and insert it at D. Continue making half cross stitches to the end of the row. Work back, stitching G to D, E to B, C to H to complete the crosses. Work further rows, until the whole area is covered. Then bring the needle out at I, and insert it at J, bringing it back out at K.

2 Work K to L and M to N to make a row of half crosses across the original crosses. Then work back across the row, stitching O to L, M to J and K to P to complete the second row of crosses that make up the stars. Work the remaining rows in the same way.

Chessboard Filling

Chessboard filling is worked over blocks of nine strands, each block being worked with three bands of satin stitch. The stitches are pulled tight to create three bars, and as the blocks are worked in alternate directions a lattice effect is created. This pattern is used in the Cupcake Apron (see page 136).

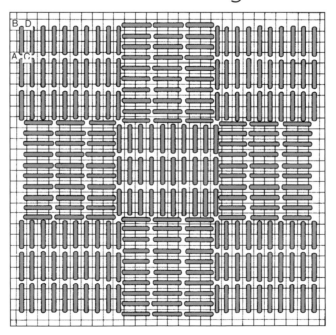

1 Bring the needle out at A and insert it three fabric strands up at B, top left of the design area. Work satin stitch (see page 135) to complete a row of ten vertical stitches. Pull each stitch tightly. Work the next row right to left directly beneath the first, so that the stitches share the holes of the satin stitches above. Work the third row left to right in the same way. Work the next block down of three satin stitch rows vertically, turning the work if this is easier. Work the next block horizontally, and so on, to fill the design area.

Diagonal Raised Band Filling

Diagonal raised band filling creates a very open effect, similar to the look of filet crochet. It is worked in a series of diagonal crosses, each stitch being firmly pulled to achieve the final effect.

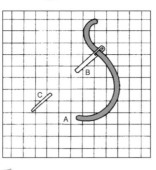

1 Bring the needle out at A, insert it at B, four strands up, and bring it out at C, two strands to the left and two strands up from A.

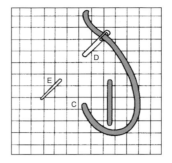

2 Insert the needle at D, four fabric strands up, and bring it out at E. Continue working the first row to cover the design area from bottom right to top left.

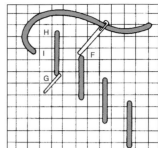

3 After completing the last stitch at H, bring the needle out at I. Insert it at F and bring it out at G to start making the crosses.

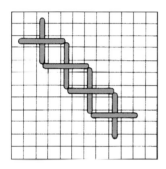

4 Complete all the crosses, pulling each stitch tight as you go.

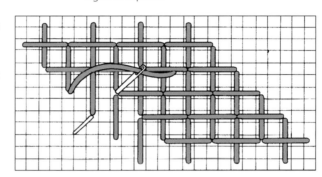

5 Work the next diagonal row of crosses so it touches the first, as shown.

Diagonal Satin Filling

Diagonal satin filling pulls the fabric to create a pattern of large and small holes with dense blocks of satin stitch between them. Blocks can also be worked in any other formation – singly, in rows or groups. This pattern is used in the Cupcake Apron (see page 136).

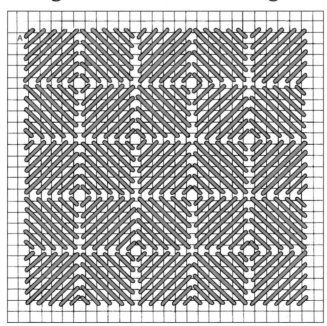

1 Bring the needle out at A at the top left of the design area and work a block of satin stitch (see page 135), working the stitches diagonally over an area of five by five fabric strands, as shown. Work the next block to the right with the stitches slanting in the opposite direction. Continue in this way, alternating the direction of stitches for each block. Stitches must be firmly pulled to achieve the effect.

Diamond Eyelet

Diamond eyelet is formed by working a series of satin stitches (see page 135) around a central hole in a diamond shape. The tighter you pull the stitches, the larger the eyelet hole becomes, so decide what effect you want before you begin. These eyelets are used in the Diamond Bracelet (see page 128).

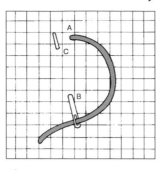

1 Bring the needle out at A, insert it at B, where the centre of the eyelet will be, and bring it out again at C.

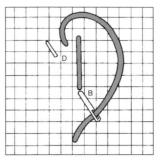

2 Insert the needle at B again and bring it out at D, as shown.

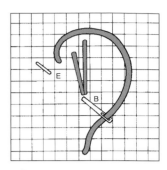

3 Insert the needle at B and bring it out at E.

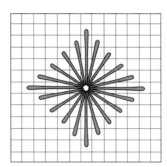

4 Continue working in this sequence around the central hole, B, to complete the diamond eyelet.

Outlined Diamond Eyelet Filling

Outlined diamond eyelet filling is worked by stitching a diamond eyelet (see above) surrounded by diagonal satin stitches (see page 135). When worked in a contrast thread, this produces an ornate look reminiscent of Indian shisha work.

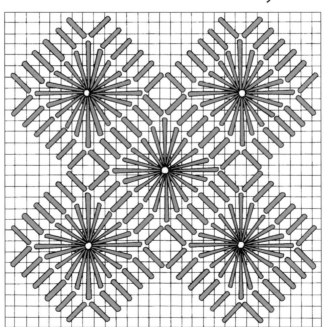

1 Work the eyelets first, following the instructions above, then work the outline in satin stitch in the same way as for mosaic filling (see page 131). Here, the eyelet is shown worked over ten fabric strands, with the diagonal satin stitches worked over two intersections.

Diamond Filling

Diamond filling is produced by working double backstitch (see below) in stepped lines to make zigzag rows. Two zigzag rows are worked to form a diamond pattern, which covers a large area quite quickly. This pattern is used in the Diamond Bracelet (see page 128).

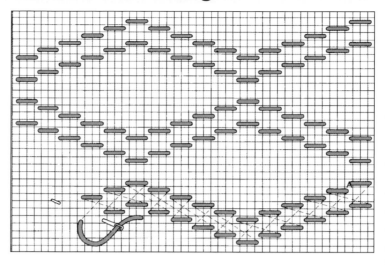

1 Begin at A on the lower right of the design area, working over the same number of fabric strands throughout. The broken lines in the diagram indicate the thread lying on the back of the fabric. The proportions of the diamonds can be varied by lengthening or shortening the zigzag lines. Pull stitches firmly for an open effect.

Double Backstitch

Double backstitch is a useful stitch because it can be viewed from both sides. On the front it creates parallel lines of backstitch, while on the back it resembles a close herringbone.

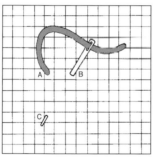

1 Bring the needle out at A and insert it at B, two fabric strands to the right. Bring it out at C, below A and four strands down.

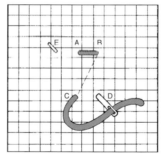

2 Insert the needle at D, in line with both B and C, and bring it out at E, level with A.

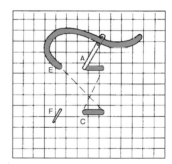

3 Insert the needle at A and bring it out at F.

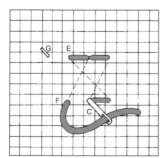

4 Insert the needle at C and bring it out at G. Continue repeating Steps 3 and 4 to complete the line.

Double Faggot Filling

Double faggot filling re-creates the look of filet lace when worked in a matching thread, but can also be worked in a colour. Its name comes from the word faggot, meaning bundle of fire wood, because the small straight stitches are bundled or grouped to make the design.

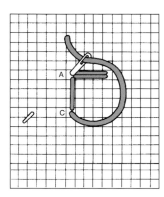

1 Bring the needle out at A, insert it at B, four fabric strands to the right, and bring it back out at A.

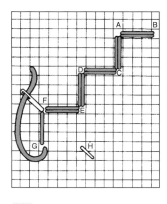

2 Insert the needle at B again and bring it out at C, four strands below A.

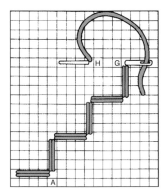

3 Insert the needle at A and bring it out at C.

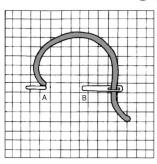

4 Re-insert the needle at A and bring it out at D.

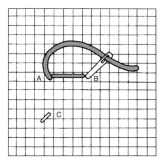

5 Continue in this way, following the alphabetical sequence to the end of the diagonal row. Bring the needle out at H and turn the work upside down.

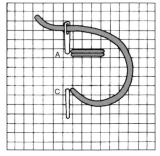

6 Insert the needle at G and bring it back out at H. Continue as before to create a diagonal row of squares. Work subsequent rows in the same way.

filet lace

This is a form of lace that consists of decorative stitches worked onto a fine, knotted net. The net is traditionally hand-made and it's thought that this type of lace was originally made by the wives of fishermen. Today the net can be made by machine (though there are still traditional hand-makers) and then you just have to frame it up in order to stitch the filet patterns.

Four-Sided Stitch

Four-sided stitch produces a close, fine, net-like effect that can look particularly delicate but is really very simple to work. It is similar in effect to double faggot filling (see opposite), except that each stitch is worked only once and a full square is completed at every stage.

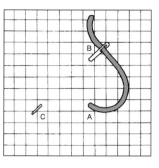

1 Bring the needle out at A and insert it at B, four fabric strands up. Bring it out at C, four strands to the left of A, as shown.

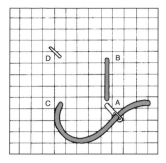

2 Insert the needle at A and bring it out at D, four strands above C.

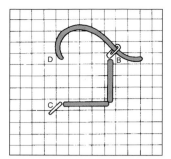

3 Insert the needle at B and bring it out at C again. Then complete the stitch by inserting the needle at D.

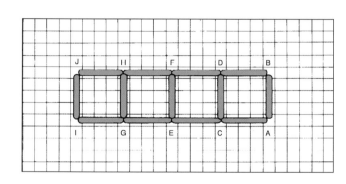

4 In a row of stitches the final stitch of the first square becomes the first stitch of the second square and so on. Work from right to left. When working subsequent rows, work back over the lower edge of the blocks above to create double horizontal lines in the same way as you create double vertical lines in the variation below.

Four-Sided Stitch Variation

This variation of four-sided stitch (see above) has staggered rows that pull the strands into scallops. It exemplifies how with pulled thread work the art lies in the positioning of basic stitches, rather than in the complicated manipulation of the threads.

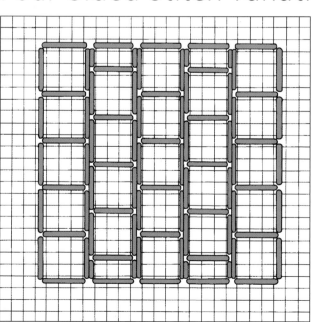

1 Work a row of four-sided stitch – in this case it is shown as a vertical row, but it can be worked horizontally. For the next row, begin and end with a half stitch worked over two-by-four fabric strands instead of the usual four-by-four strands. Work a standard row followed by another row with half stitches at each end, and so on until the design area is filled.

Diamond bracelet

Simple to sew, this is an elegant accessory that has the distinct advantage of being much less expensive than real diamonds. Here, it's made in the traditional pulled thread palette of white-on-white, but you can, of course, make your bracelet in whatever colours you choose. Pale green fabric with bright green embroidery would make lovely emeralds…

MATERIALS
- Tape measure
- Two pieces of 35-count evenweave fabric in antique white measuring 30 x 12cm (12 x 4¾in)
- Tacking thread
- Hand-sewing needle
- 20cm (8in) ring frame
- Diamond bracelet chart (see page 173)
- Anchor Stranded Cotton: one skein in colour 2
- Size 26 tapestry needle
- Pins
- Fading fabric marker
- Sewing thread to match fabric
- Sewing machine
- Pinking shears
- Small, sharp scissors
- Piece of 1.5-cm (⅝-in) wide organza ribbon measuring 65cm (25in) long

STITCHES USED
- Diamond eyelet (see page 124)
- Diamond filling (see page 125)

THE EMBROIDERY
Tack a cross on one piece of fabric to establish the centre (see page 20), then fix the fabric into the ring frame (see page 18). The chart shows an eyelet and two repeats of the diamond pattern: starting at the centre of the fabric, count out to one side the number of strands you require to work the number of diamonds needed (see Getting It Right, below). Embroider the diamond pattern either side of the tacked centre line. Count the number of fabric strands to the position of the eyelet and work one at each end of the line of diamonds.

MAKING UP
Right sides facing, tack the two pieces of fabric together, stitching in a rectangle about 1cm (⅜in) outside the edges of the embroidery. Using the fading fabric marker, draw a wavy-edged box outside the tacked rectangle, this will be the shape of the bracelet. Don't make the curves too tight or they will be difficult to turn right side out neatly. Set the sewing machine to a small straight stitch and, sewing slowly and carefully, sew around the drawn line, leaving a 5cm (2in) gap in one long side for turning through.

Using pinking shears, trim the fabric to 5mm (¼in) outside the stitching. Using small, sharp scissors, very carefully snip notches in the seam allowances around all the curves, cutting to within 2mm (⅛in) of the stitches. Turn the bracelet right side out through the gap, making sure all the curves are turned out smoothly. Press the bracelet, pressing under the seam allowances across the gap. Slip stitch the gap closed.

Put the tapestry needle into the hole of one eyelet and use it to push apart the strands of the backing fabric to create a hole for the ribbon to pass through: the ribbon is fine and narrow, so the hole can be very small. Repeat at the other end, thread the ribbon through both ends of the bracelet and tie in a bow.

getting it right

Measure your wrist and decide how long you want your bracelet to be. The bracelet shown here is 21.5cm (8½in) long, but can be adjusted by embroidering one diamond more or fewer: each diamond is approximately 2cm (¾in) long. The eyelets at each end extend the bracelet by a further 2cm (¾in) each, and there is approximately 1.5cm (⅝in) of fabric beyond the eyelet at each end.

Greek Cross Stitch Lacy Filling

Greek cross stitches can be worked individually or in patterns as a filling stitch. Two commonly used patterns are lacy filling, shown here, and the squared variation (see below). This pattern is used in the Cupcake Apron (see page 136).

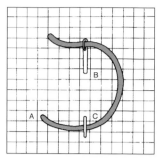

1 Bring the needle out at A, insert it at B, four fabric strands up and four strands to the right, and bring it back out at C, keeping the thread under the needle, as shown.

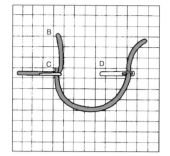

2 Pull the thread through and insert the needle at D, four strands to the right, bringing it out again at C and keeping the thread under the needle.

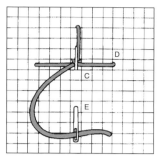

3 Pull the thread through and insert the needle at E, four strands down, bringing it out again at C.

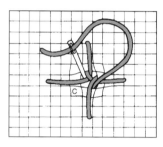

4 Pull the thread through and secure the cross by inserting the needle again at C, overlapping the last and first stitches.

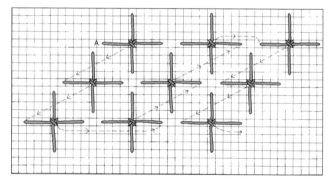

5 For lacy filling, work each Greek cross over the same number of strands. Start the sequence at A. The broken lines indicate the direction of the connecting thread between stitches on the reverse side. Work diagonal rows.

Greek Cross Stitch Squared Filling

This squared filling of Greek cross stitch is worked in diagonal rows, set so that the crosses form large squares. Work each stitch over the same number of strands.

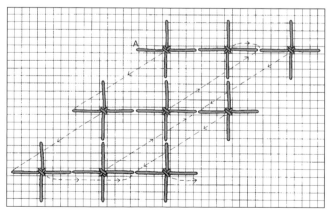

1 Following the diagram, begin the first stitch at A and work the crosses, as above, in diagonal rows. The broken lines indicate the direction of the connecting thread between stitches on the reverse side. On completion of the first diagonal row, turn the fabric and work the next diagonal row back beside the first one. Work subsequent rows in the same way.

Honeycomb Filling

Honeycomb filling, as its name suggests, creates a honeycomb effect. This is more pronounced when the stitch is worked in a thread that will show up on the fabric; either a contrast colour or a darker shade of the fabric colour. This filling is used in the Cupcake Apron (see page 136).

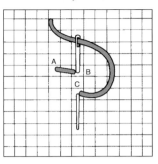 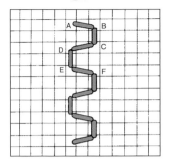 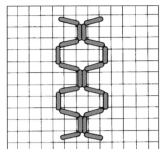

1 Bring the needle out at A, insert it at B, two fabric strands to the right, and bring it out at C, two strands down. Insert the needle at B and bring it out at C again.

2 Continue as shown, inserting the needle at D, bringing it out at E, inserting it at D again and back out at E, inserting it at F, and so on.

3 To work a second row position the stitches as shown, working the connecting stitches into shared holes. Repeat these two rows to fill a design area.

Mosaic Filling

Mosaic filling is perfect for geometric designs as its squared format really comes into its own. It can be used individually or in blocks for borders. It is easier to work than it may appear, comprising satin stitch (see page 135) with four-sided stitch (see page 127) and cross stitch (see page 23).

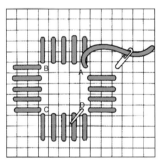 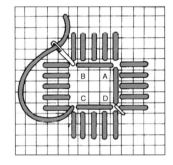 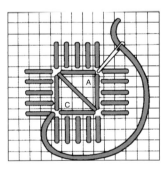

1 Starting at A and working to the left, work five satin stitches over three fabric strands to form a block. Bring the needle out at B and work the next block vertically. Work four blocks altogether to form a square, as shown. On completion of the last stitch, bring the needle through at D.

2 Work a four-sided stitch, then bring the needle through again at D.

3 Stitch diagonally across the central square. Bring the needle out at C and insert it at A to complete the central cross stitch.

Punch Stitch

Punch stitch is very similar to four-sided stitch (see page 127) in effect, but in this case the stitches are worked twice for greater impact.

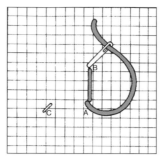 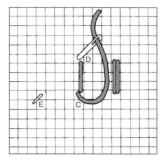 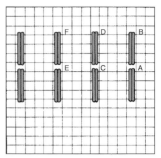

1 Bring the needle out at A, insert it at B, four fabric strands up, and bring it out again at A. Insert the needle again at B and bring it out at C, four strands down and four strands to the left.

2 Insert the needle at D, four strands up, and bring it out again at C, then insert the needle at D and bring it out at E. Continue working in this way for the required length.

3 Turn the fabric to work the next row, as shown. Work all the rows required to fill the area.

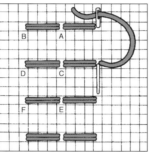

4 To complete the squares, turn the fabric sideways and work the stitches in the same way.

Spaced Satin Filling

Spaced satin filling pulls the fabric into distinct ripples or waves. The blocks of satin stitch (see page 135) are arranged in a chequerboard pattern and the stitches are pulled tightly.

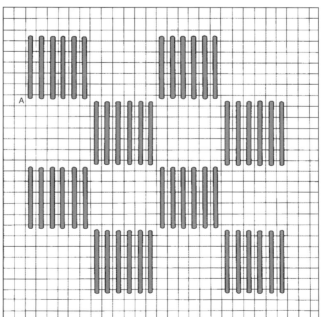

1 Beginning at A, work the first row of satin stitch blocks vertically or horizontally. Work the second row of blocks so that they are positioned between the blocks of the first row. Continue working rows of blocks as shownin the diagram to fill the space.

Step Filling

Step filling is worked like spaced satin filling (see opposite, below), except that the blocks run in alternate directions. This simple change gives this stitch a completely different look – that of a woven effect.

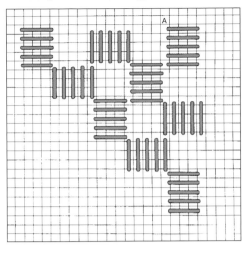

1 Beginning at A, work diagonal lines of satin stitch blocks (see page 135), with five stitches to a block and each block worked over four strands. Work one diagonal line with the satin stitches running horizontally, then work a diagonal line with the stitches running vertically and so on. All the stitches must be pulled firmly to achieve the desired effect.

Wave Stitch

Wave stitch is worked by making a series of connecting diagonal straight stitches that pull the fabric into a herringbone pattern of holes. When worked in a contrasting thread the diagonal lines of stitching become more prominent. It is used in the Cupcake Apron (see page 136).

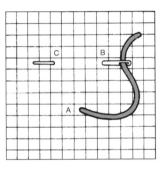

1 Bring the needle out at A, insert it at B, four fabric strands up and two strands to the right, and bring it back out at C, four strands to the left.

2 Insert the needle at A and bring it out at D, four strands to the left.

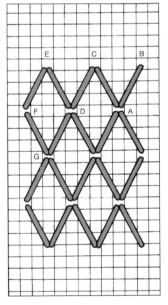

3 Insert the needle at C and bring it out at E, four strands to the left. Continue in this way to the end of the row.

4 To start the second row, complete the stitch F to E and bring the needle out at G. Insert the needle at F, four strands up and two strands to the left, and bring it out at D. Continue stitching in the same sequence to make the pattern shown.

Florentine Stitch

Florentine stitch is created by working straight stitches in staggered formation (see also page 141). The stitches are not pulled tight and the pattern complements pulled work beautifully. This stitch is used in the Cupcake Apron (see page 136).

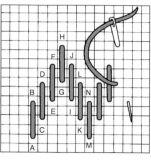

1 Bring the needle out at A and insert it at B, four fabric strands up (though this can be six strands). Bring the needle out at C, halfway between A and B and one strand to the right, and insert it at D, four or six strands up. Work in an up and down sequence to make the pattern, as shown.

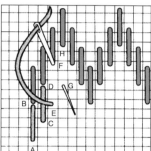

2 Work the next line of stitching immediately below the first, with the stitches sharing some holes.

French Knots

French knots are small, decorative knots worked on the right side of the fabric. They are common to many syles of embroidery and, in the context of pulled thread work, are used in the Cupcake Apron (see page 136).

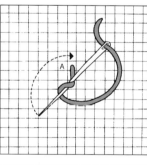

1 Bring the needle out at A, at the knot position. Twist the thread once or twice around the needle, depending on the size of knot required.

2 Holding the wraps in place, insert the needle one fabric strand away from A and pull the thread through to form the knot. Secure the knot on the wrong side by taking a small catching stitch under nearby embroidery threads.

Holbein Stitch

Holbein stitch is also known as double running stitch and is one of the easiest and most satisfying of the outline stitches. All you do is work evenly-spaced running stitch and fill in the gaps on the return journey. It looks the same on both sides and therefore was traditionally used to decorate items that might be viewed from the 'wrong' side.

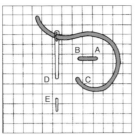

1 Bring the needle out at A, at the start of the line. Insert the needle at B and bring it out at C. Insert the needle at D and bring it out at E. Continue in this way.

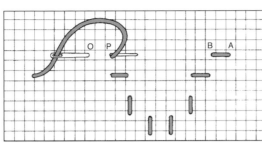

2 When you reach the end of the design line, bring the needle back out at the start of the final stitch, as shown.

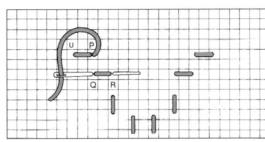

3 Work back along the line, filling in the spaces between the existing stitches. The design line can be straight or can twist and turn as desired.

Satin Stitch

Satin stitch is the basis of many pulled thread patterns and no stitching repertoire would be complete without it.

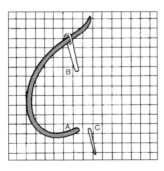

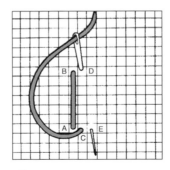

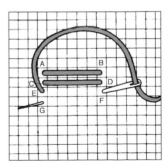

1 For vertical satin stitch, bring the needle out at A at the base of the shape and insert it at B at the top of the shape, bringing it out again at C, next to A.

2 Continue to work parallel stitches in this way.

3 Satin stitch can be worked in any direction, even diagonally. The direction of stitches has a major impact on the final effect of the pattern, so always think about which way to work it before you begin.

Cupcake apron

So very sweet, this little apron will make anyone feel like a domestic goddess. These fabrics have a very retro, 1950s flavour, and the colours echo those in the cupcakes, though you could pick out the greens or yellows instead.

MATERIALS

- Two pieces of 35-count evenweave fabric in antique white measuring 20 x 20cm (8 x 8in)
- Tacking thread
- Hand-sewing needle
- Tape measure
- Ring frame
- Fading fabric marker
- Cupcake charts (see page 173)
- Anchor Stranded Cotton: one skein each of colours 27, 29, 40, 186, 240, 276, 278, 279, 907 and 1012
- Size 26 tapestry and size 12 embroidery needle
- Scissors
- Two pieces of medium-weight white cotton fabric measuring 16 x 15cm (6¼ x 6in)
- Pins
- Sewing thread to match fabrics and ric-rac
- Sewing machine
- Piece of medium-weight cotton fabric measuring 60 x 55cm (24 x 22in)
- Ric-rac measuring 170cm (67in) long
- Two pieces of medium-weight cotton fabric measuring 150 x 11cm (59 x 4½in) – the first measurement should be long enough to go around your waist and tie in a bow
- Iron
- Piece of medium-weight iron-on interfacing measuring 50 x 11cm (20 x 4½in)

STITCHES USED

- Chessboard filling (see page 122)
- Diagonal satin filling (see page 123)
- Florentine stitch (see page 134)
- French knots (see page 134)
- Greek cross stitch lacy filling (see page 130)
- Honeycomb filling (see page 131)
- Stem stitch (see page 101)
- Tent stitch (see page 140)
- Wave stitch (see page 133)

THE EMBROIDERY

Tack a cross on both pieces of evenweave fabric to establish the centre (see page 20). Fix one piece in a ring frame (see page 18) and use the fading fabric marker to transfer the outline of the cupcake onto the fabric (see page 12). Following the chart, embroider the cupcake. Work all the pulled stitch patterns first using two strands of thread throughout. At the edges of shapes, work shorter stitches to keep the outline smooth if need be, as indicated on the chart. Once these are complete, use the embroidery needle and two strands of thread to work the French knots.

Repeat the process to embroider the fairy cake onto the other piece of fabric. Once the pulled thread stitches are complete, use the embroidery needle and two strands of thread to work stem stitch outlines around the fairy wings, and the straight stitches.

Remove all tacking stitches.

MAKING UP

Cut the embroideries down to 16 x 15cm (6¼ x 6in), with the design approximately 4cm (1½in) in from the sides and bottom and 5cm (2in) down from the top. Pin the wrong side of one embroidery to the right side of a piece of white fabric, matching all edges. Set the sewing machine to a small zigzag stitch and sew the layers together all around. Press under a 1cm (⅜in) hem on the bottom and side edges. On the top edge, press under a 5mm (¼in) hem then a 1cm (⅜in) hem. Repeat with the other piece of embroidery and white fabric, then set these aside; they will be the pockets.

Establish one long straight edge of the large piece of fabric as the top, then draw around a saucer to round off the two bottom corners. Turn under and press a double 1cm (⅜in) hem along the two side and the bottom edges, pleating the hem on the rounded corners so that it lies flat. Set the sewing machine to a small straight stitch and sew the hem.

Pin and then tack the ric-rac around the hemmed edge of the apron: it is worth tacking as ric-rac does tend to try and wriggle while being stitched on. Machine-sew the ric-rac in place, sewing down the centre of it.

Position the pockets on the apron, placing each one approximately 16cm (6¼in) up from the bottom edge and 11cm (4½in) in from the side. Pin then tack them in place. Sewing as close as possible to the edge, sew each pocket to the apron, pivoting neatly at the bottom corners and reversing a couple of times at the top edge for strength.

Set the sewing machine to the longest straight stitch and loosen the tension. Sew a line across the top of the fabric, 1cm (⅜in) from the edge. Gently pull on both ends of the bobbin thread to gather up the fabric to about 38cm (15¼in), or the desired width. Tie the ends of the spool and bobbin threads together to secure the gathers.

Following the manufacturer's instructions, iron the interfacing to the middle of the wrong side of the long strip of fabric. Press under 1cm (⅜in) along each edge of this strip, then press it in half lengthways. Mark the centre of the waistband strip and the centre of the gathered top edge of the apron with pins. Matching the centres, slip 2.5cm (1in) of the gathered edge into the folded waistband and pin it in place. Pin the open edges of the rest of the waistband strip together. Set the sewing machine to a medium straight stitch and the tension back to a balanced one. Sewing very close to the pinned edge, sew down one short end, right along the long edge – sewing the gathered apron edge in place as you go – and up the other short end.

CANVASWORK

Canvaswork is one of the most popular types of embroidery in the world. The most commonly seen form is needlepoint, where designs (usually printed on the canvas) are worked in tent stitch. Brilliant designers have created fantastic needlepoint kits that are a delight to stitch, but if you explore further there is a lot more to canvaswork than tent stitch.

Canvaswork is worked on, as the name suggests, canvas, and the stitches can be made in all kinds of threads and wools. As long as the thread fits easily through the holes in the canvas and no canvas shows when the stitching is complete, you can use whatever materials you like. For general instructions for preparing fabric, transferring a design and starting and finishing stitching, turn to pages 14–22.

To encourage exploration, the two projects in this chapter both avoid needlepoint. The Bargello Cushion (see page 146) is worked in a traditional flame pattern, while the jaunty Bunting Clutch Purse (see page 154), a perfect summer accessory, makes good use of a range of stitches.

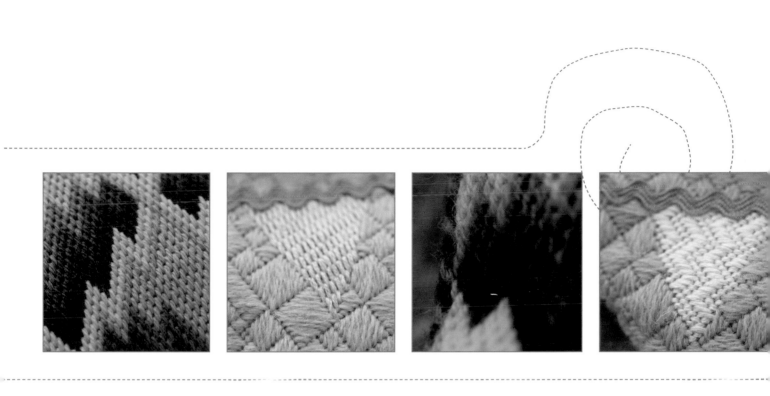

Tent Stitch

Tent stitch is the most commonly used stitch in canvaswork, so it has been listed first in this chapter (the other stitches are listed alphabetically). Tent stitch is used to fill in edges of pennants in the Bunting Clutch Purse (see page 154), where the pattern stitch does not quite fill the shape.

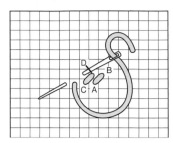

1 To work in horizontal rows, start the first row on the right-hand side and work towards the left. Bring the needle out at A and insert it at B, one canvas strand up and to the right of A. Bring the needle out at C, next to A, and insert it at D, next to B. Continue in this way to the end of the row.

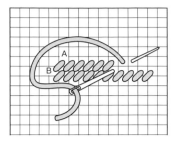

2 To work the next row, running in the opposite direction, bring the needle out at A and insert it at B, and so on.

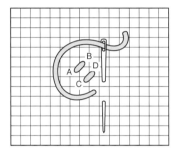

1 To work in diagonal rows, bring the needle out at A and insert it at B. Bring the needle out at C, two canvas strands below B and insert it at D. Note that there is a free hole on the diagonal line between the stitches. Continue in this way.

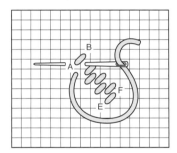

2 To work the next row, bring the needle out at E and insert it at F. Work along the row with the needle being inserted into the holes left between stitches in the previous row.

Half Cross Stitch

Half cross stitch looks the same as tent stitch, but does not cover the canvas as well, although it does use less thread. It shouldn't be mixed with tent stitch as the surface of the embroidery will be uneven.

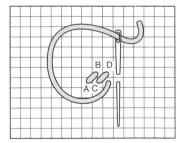

1 Bring the needle out at A and insert it at B, one canvas strand up and to the right of A. Bring it out at C, one strand below B, and insert it at D, next to B. Subsequent rows will be worked the same way, but with the work progressing in the opposite direction.

Bargello Stitch

Bargello stitch is sometimes called Florentine stitch or flame stitch. It consists simply of straight stitches, worked over a varying number of canvas strands, depending on the pattern required (here it is worked over four strands). The Bargello Cushion (see page 146) is worked with this stitch.

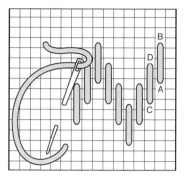

1 The first row of stitches will set the pattern, so ensure it is worked correctly. Bring the needle out at A, insert it at B, bring it out at C and insert it again at D. Continue in this way until the first pattern row is completed.

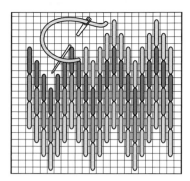

2 Subsequent rows can be worked over the same number of canvas strands or a different number, as the pattern requires. Each row follows the shaping of the first row, with the needle coming out of a hole shared with a previous stitch. The pattern shown here is a simple, classic zigzag.

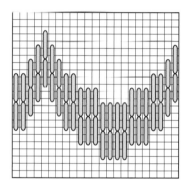

3 Curves can be achieved by working several stitches on the same level in a row. These curves can be combined with sharp points to increase the pattern complexity.

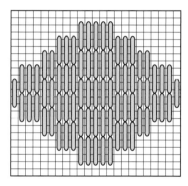

4 Motifs are symmetrical and can be incorporated into a zigzag or curve pattern. Inner rows an be worked over a different number of strands to outer rows, but the pattern needs to be carefully worked out.

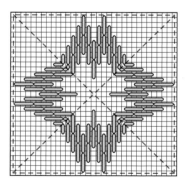

5 Four-way bargello is a radiating design made up of four identical sections. Draw or tack a line around the outer edge of the design and two diagonal crossing lines, as shown by the red lines in the illustration. Establish the first row of the pattern in one section, working from the middle out to one edge, and then from the middle out to the other edge. Work the same row in each section to ensure the pattern joins up. Then work the subsequent rows. Some smaller stitches will be needed to fill in gaps in the corners and middle of a pattern.

Brick Stitch

Brick stitch is an easy filling stitch that will cover a large area quickly. Rows can be worked in varying tones for a subtly shaded effect.

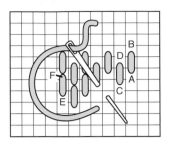

1 Bring the needle out at A on the left-hand side and insert it two canvas strands up at B. Bring it out three strands below and one to the left at C and insert it at D. Repeat these two stitches to the end of the row. Work back in the opposite direction, bringing the needle out at E and inserting it at F, and so on.

Byzantine Stitch

Byzantine stitch is shown here worked over two intersections in the canvas, but the stitches can be longer if desired. This stitch is used in a pennant in the Bunting Clutch Purse (see page 154).

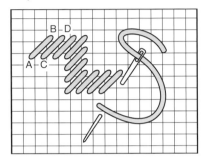

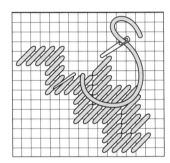

1 The first row is worked from left to right. Bring the needle out at A, insert it at B, bring it out at C and insert it again at D. Work two more stitches in the same way to produce four in a row. Then work two stitches immediately below the fourth stitch. Work the next row of four, starting the first stitch immediately below the two just worked. Continue in this way until the first row has crossed the design area.

2 The next row is worked from right to left, with the stitches covering the same number of intersections and fitting into the pattern established by the first row.

Cashmere Stitch

Cashmere stitch is a popular filling stitch that gives small-scale texture to larger areas. It features in a pennant in the Bunting Clutch Purse (see page 154).

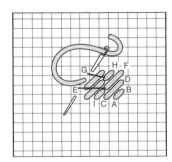

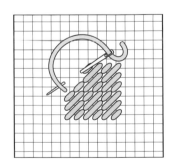

1 Each block is made up of four stitches. Work the first block on the right of the design area, bringing the needle out at A and inserting it one canvas strand up and to the right at B, on the edge of the design. Bring it out at C, inserting it at D, then E–F and G–H. Start the second block to the left, bringing the needle out at I and inserting it at E. Work blocks across the row.

2 Work the second row from right to left again, turning the work if this is easier. The rows of blocks sit above one another, forming a chequered pattern.

Double Cross Stitch

Double cross stitch combines slanting crosses (see page 23) with small upright crosses (see page 144) to create a very textural stitch. The top threads of both types of cross should lie in the same direction.

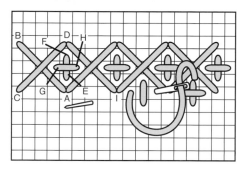

1 Work the first slanting cross on the left of the design area, bringing the needle out at A and inserting it four canvas strands up and four strands to the left at B, then making the second stitch from C to D. Work the first upright cross to the right, stitching E–F, over two strands, then G–H. Bring the needle out at I to start the second slanting cross. Work the next row of upright crosses only from right to left, as shown. Then start the complete sequence again from the left.

Italian Cross Stitch

Italian cross stitch creates a dense texture that fills small areas well, but can look very busy in large areas. Each row is worked in two sequences, first from right to left then from left to right.

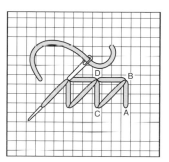

1 Bring the needle out at A on the left-hand side of the design area and insert it at B. Bring it out at C and insert it at B again to make the slanting stitch, then bring it out at D and insert it at B again to complete this part of the block. Bring the needle out at C to start the next block to the right.

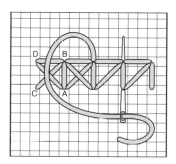

2 Bring the needle out at point D of the last block worked and insert it at point A to complete the cross. Bring it out at point B to start the slanting stitch to complete the next cross to the right. Start the next row from the left so the first D–B stitch completes the squares of the first row.

Long-Arm Cross Stitch

Long-arm cross stitch creates a plaited effect when worked in rows. It's a quick stitch to work and is useful for describing woven textures.

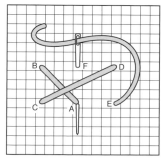

1 Bring the needle out at A and insert it at B, on the left-hand edge of the design area. Bring it out at C, four canvas strands below B, and insert it at D, level with B and four strands to the right of A, to create the long arm of the cross. To work the next cross to the right, bring the needle out at E, four strands below D, and insert it at F, so that this short arm of the second cross crosses the long arm of the first cross. Work all the rows from left to right in this way.

Upright Cross Stitch

Upright cross stitch is another variation of the classic cross. All the top threads of the crosses should lie in the same direction, with the horizontal one usually being on top, as here.

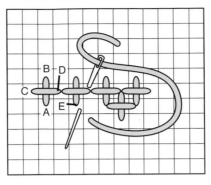

1 Bring the needle out at A and insert it two canvas strands above at B, then bring it out at C on the left-hand edge of the design area and insert it two strands to the right at D to complete the cross. Start the next cross to the right at E. Work the next row from right to left, fitting the crosses into the gaps between those in the first row, as shown.

Cushion Stitch

Cushion stitch is excellent for describing architecture in a design. It's also useful as a textural background stitch and is used this way in the Bunting Clutch Purse (see page 154).

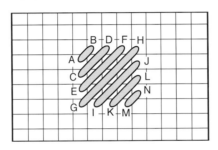

1 Each cushion is made up of a series of slanting stitches arranged in a square. Here, there are seven stitches worked over a square that is four strands in each direction. However, blocks can be any size and can be rectangular. To work the one shown, bring the needle out at A and insert it at B, bring it out at C and insert it at D, then work E–F, G–H, I–J, K–L and M–N.

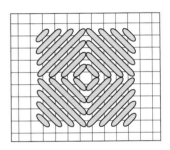

2 Blocks slanting in different directions can be fitted together to make a larger block, as shown.

Crossed Cushion Stitch

Crossed cushion stitch offers a way of adding further texture to cushion stitch (see above). The crossing stitches should be worked at right angles to the underlying stitches, but can cover any half of the square.

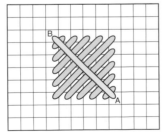

1 Bring the needle out at A and insert it at B. If desired, just this single stitch can be left crossing the cushion.

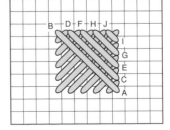

2 To cover half a cushion, continue stitching C–D, E–F, G–H and I–J.

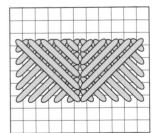

3 Crossed blocks can be worked slanting in different direction to make up geometric patterns.

Darning Stitch

Darning stitch produces a ribbed texture that is effective but quite slow to work, so best used on small or medium areas.

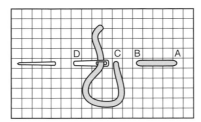

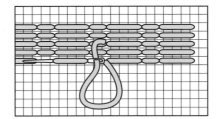

1 Bring the needle out at A on the right-hand side of the design area. Make a stitch over four canvas strands to B. Bring the needle out two strands along at C and continue the row in this way.

2 Turn the work if that is easier and stitch back across the row, filling in the gaps. Be careful not to pierce the previous stitch when inserting the needle in a shared hole.

Circular Eyelet

Circular eyelets resemble tiny flowers when massed together. They can be worked in one colour, as in a pennant in the Bunting Clutch Purse (see page 154), or a variety of colours for spotted effect.

1 Bring the needle out at A and insert it three canvas strands to the left at B, the centre of the eyelet. Bring the needle out at C and insert it again at B. Work in a clockwise direction to make all 16 spokes of the eyelet, inserting the needle at B each time.

2 To make the next eyelet to the left, bring the needle out at the end of the J spoke of the previous eyelet and insert it three strands to the left in what will be the centre of the new eyelet. Subsequent rows of eyelets fit between the spokes of previous ones, as shown.

Diamond Eyelet

Diamond eyelets are a variation of the circular eyelet and they tessellate very neatly together. Use them as a filling, or work individual eyelets surrounded by a simple stitch such as tent stitch (see page 140).

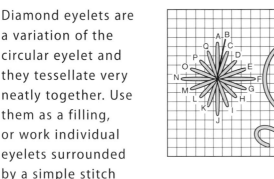

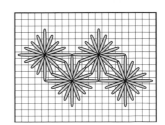

1 Bring the needle out at A and insert it four canvas strands below at B, the centre of the eyelet. Bring the needle out at C and insert it again at B. Work in a clockwise direction to make all 16 spokes of the eyelet, inserting the needle at B each time. To start the next eyelet, bring the needle out at R, eight strands to the right of A, and take it down four strands below at S.

2 Subsequent rows of eyelets fit between the spokes of previous ones, as shown.

Bargello cushion

Once you've established the first row of the pattern, stitching this cushion cover is so easy. As the canvas is a large gauge, the wool quite chunky and each stitch covers four strands of canvas, the design 'grows' quickly. I used the simplest method of making up the cushion cover, so this really is a great project for a novice embroiderer and sewer.

MATERIALS

- Piece of 14-count canvas measuring 50 x 40cm (20 x 16in)
- Slate frame or roller frame
- Tape measure
- Bargello chart (see page 173)
- Anchor Tapisserie Wool: five skeins of colour 8018, four skeins of 8586, three skeins of 8590, four skeins of 8592, six skeins of 8596 and three skeins of 9790
- Size 22 tapestry needle
- Scissors
- Piece of chenille (or other furnishing weight fabric) measuring 43 x 33cm (17 x 13in)
- Pins
- Sewing machine
- Sewing thread to match fabric
- Iron
- Cushion pad measuring 40 x 30cm (16 x 12in)
- Hand-sewing needle
- Furnishing cord (optional)

STITCHES USED

- Bargello stitch (see page 141)

THE EMBROIDERY

Fix the canvas into a slate frame or roller frame (see pages 18–19). Tacking along the weave of the canvas, tack a rectangle measuring 40 x 30cm (16 x 12in) to define the embroidery area, then tack a centred cross to establish the middle (see page 20). Following the chart and using a single strand of wool, start by stitching one motif centrally on the canvas. Working out to one side, stitch the upper line of more motifs until you reach the edge of the tacked rectangle. Work out to the other side in the same way, ensuring that the design ends symmetrically. Fill in the rest of these motifs. Then fill the lower half of the rectangle with motifs, and finally fill in the upper half (as the motif is not symmetrical top to bottom, the design will not finish at the same point on the top and bottom edges of the tacked rectangle). Remove the tacking stitches.

MAKING UP

Take the fabric out of the slate frame and cut the embroidery, cutting 2cm (¾in) outside the stitching. Using the sewing machine, zigzag stitch around the edge of the canvas.

Right sides facing, pin the canvas and fabric together. Set the sewing machine to a small straight stitch and put the cushion cover canvas-side up under the needle. Position it so that the needle will stitch into the row of canvas holes that the embroidery finishes in. Starting on one short edge 4cm (1½in) from the corner, sew carefully up to the corner and around the edges, stopping 4cm (1½in) after the last corner so that there is a gap in the middle of one short side. Remove the pins. Cut off the corners of the canvas and fabric, cutting 5mm (¼in) from the stitching. Turn the cover right side out, making sure the corners are turned out smoothly. Press under the seam allowance on the fabric across the gap and finger-press the seam allowance on the canvas.

Measure around the edges of the cushion and add 30 per cent to this measurement. Cut four lengths of yarn to this measurement, two lengths of two colours. Knot all four lengths together at one end and ask a friend to hold the knot. Divide the yarns into two groups, one group of each colour. Start to twist the ends of the yarns, twisting each group in the same direction. When the yarns are so twisted that they are beginning to kink, ask your friend to let go of the knot. Let the cord coil up, then gently pull it out straight to produce a twisted cord. Knot the other end. Alternatively, you can buy a furnishing cord to coordinate with the yarn colours.

Insert the cushion pad into the cover and make sure all the corners of the pad are tucked into the corners of the cover. Slip stitch the gap closed, but before completing the stitching, tuck one knot of the twisted cord into the gap in the cover. Sew almost up to the cord and, leaving a tiny gap, sew the knot in place. Using sewing thread to match the yarn, sew the cord all around the cushion to cover the join between the canvas and fabric. Make a tiny stitch through the edge of the embroidered canvas, right on the seam, then make a tiny stitch through the underside of the cord, then pull the stitch tight. Continue in this way right around the cover. When you reach the start of the cord, tuck the other knot into the tiny gap remaining (tie a new knot and trim any excess cord if need be) and sew it in place to join the ends of the cord.

getting it right

I've chosen a rich palette of purples accented with bright yellow and cool grey, but you can choose any six colours you like. However, it's worth buying just one skein of each colour and testing out your palette by stitching a single motif before embarking on the whole project.

Slanted Gobelin Stitch

Slanted Gobelin stitch is a useful and popular filling stitch that will quickly cover a large area with obvious slanting lines. The stitches may be a different length to those shown here.

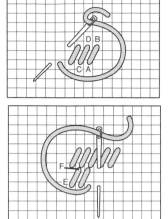

1 Bring the needle out at A and insert it at B, two strands up and one strand to the right, on the right-hand side of the design area. Bring it out at C and insert it at D, and continue in this way to the end of the row.

2 Work the next row from left to right, bringing the needle out at E and inserting it at F to make the first stitch.

Encroaching Slanted Gobelin Stitch

Encroaching slanted Gobelin stitch is a variation of slanted Gobelin stitch (see above) that can be worked in rows of toning colours to produce smoothly shaded areas. This stitch is used in a pennant in the Bunting Clutch Purse (see page 154).

1 Bring the needle out at A and insert it at B, three strands up and one strand to the right, on the right-hand side of the design area. Bring it out at C and insert it at D, and continue in this way to the end of the row.

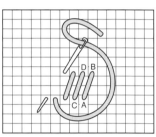

2 Work the next row from left to right. To make the first stitch, bring the needle out at E, two strands below the last stitch on the previous row, and insert it at F, one strand above the base of the last stitch on the previous row.

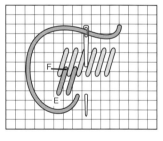

Hungarian Diamond Stitch

Hungarian diamond stitch offers a quick way of covering a large area with a defined but not fussy texture. It is featured on a pennant in the Bunting Clutch Purse (see page 154).

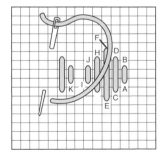

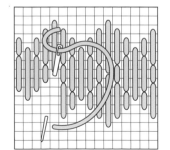

2 Work the next row of diamonds from left to right, fitting them in between those of the first row, as shown. Work the following row from right to left again.

1 Each diamond is composed of five stitches. Work the first row from right to left, bringing the needle out at A and inserting it at B. Bring it out at C and insert it at D, then work E–F, G–H and I–J to complete the diamond. Bring the needle out at K, two canvas strands to the right of I to start the next diamond in the row.

Jacquard Stitch

Jacquard stitch is a variation of Byzantine stitch (see page 142) combined with tent stitch (see page 140). Jacquard is used in one colour in a pennant in the Bunting Clutch Purse (see page 154).

1 Fill the design area with Byzantine stitches, spacing the rows one strand apart, as shown. Fill the gaps with tent stitch, working from bottom right to top left and making sure you work the stitches correctly.

Leaf Stitch

Leaf stitch can be used as an all-over background, or individual leaves can be worked and surrounded by a simple stitch such as tent stitch (see page 140). In a background the leaves can be worked in different tones to good effect.

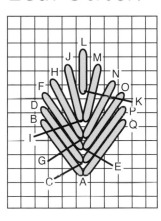

1 Starting on the left of the design area, bring the needle out at A at the base of the leaf and insert it four canvas strands up and three strands to the left at B. Work four more stitches up the left-hand side of the leaf, C–D, E–F, G–H and I–J. Work the top stitch K–L, noting that K is two strands above I. Then work down the right-hand side, working M–I, N–G, O–E, P–C and Q–A.

2 The next leaf starts six strands to the right of A of the first leaf. The next row of leaves fits between those of the first row, with the starting point nine strands below the tip of the shared B/Q hole of the first row of leaves.

Leviathan Stitch

Leviathan stitch creates chunky texture when massed together in rows. It can also be effective in bands interspersed with other, flatter stitches. This is an easy stitch as it is basically just two crosses, one on top of the other.

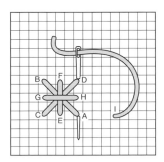

1 Bring the needle out at A and insert it at B on the left-hand side of the design area. Make a second slanting stitch from C to D to complete the underlying cross. Then work E–F and G–H to make the second cross and complete the stitch. Start the next stitch at I.

2 Work the next row from right to left, bringing the needle out at J to start the first stitch. Work the separate stitches of each leviathan stitch in the same order.

Milanese Stitch

Milanese stitch is best used over large and medium-sized areas. The diagonal lines are bold and alternate rows can be stitched in different colours to create striped or blended effects. This stitch is used on a pennant in the Bunting Clutch Purse (see page 154).

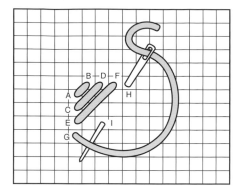

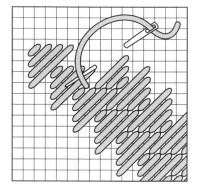

1 The stitch is composed of small triangles, each made up of four slanting stitches. Starting at the top left of the design area, bring the needle out at A and insert it at B. Bring it out at C and insert it at D, then work E to F and G to H to complete the triangle. Bring it out at I to start the next triangle.

2 Work the next row from bottom right to top left. The triangles are the same format but are inverted, each stitch sharing a hole with a stitch of the previous row, as shown.

Oriental Stitch

Oriental stitch is a variation of Milanese stitch (see above) and can be used in similar situations. The arrows can be one colour and the inserts another, as shown, or a wider range of different tones can be used.

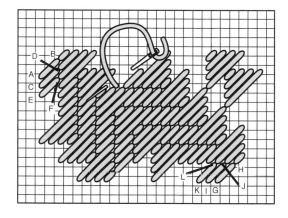

1 Work rows of Milanese stitches, spacing them so that just the longest stitches share a hole, as shown. Then fill the gaps with diagonal stitches, three in each gap. Starting at the top left, fill the gaps in the first row by bringing the needle out at A and inserting it at B, then work C–D and E–F. Working the next row in the opposite direction, bring the needle out at G and insert it at H, then work I–J and K–L.

Parisian Stitch

Parisian stitch is a great filling stitch for medium and large backgrounds. It's quick and easy to work and varying tones can be used to good effect. It is used on a pennant in the Bunting Clutch Purse (see page 154).

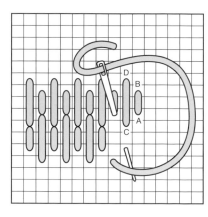

1 Bring the needle out at A on the right-hand side of the design area and insert it two canvas strands above at B. Bring it out at C, one strand below and to the left of A, and insert it four strands above at D. Repeat these two stitches across the row. Work the next row from right to left, fitting the short stitches below the long ones of the previous row and the long ones below the short ones, as shown.

Petal Stitch

Petal stitch is best worked in a finer thread, such as crewel wool (see page 10), as 20 stitches need to go through the central hole. The underlying spiral is worked until it covers the canvas, so a fine thread is good there, too.

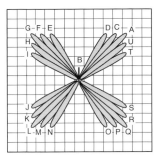

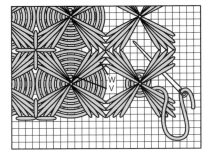

1 Start at the top right of a petal and bring the needle out at A then insert it at B. Bring it out at C and insert it again at B. Work stitches D to U as shown, inserting the needle at B each time. The next group of spokes can be worked to the right or left.

2 When all the spokes are complete, work the spirals. Bring the needle out at V and pass it under each five-stitch cluster of spokes in turn, without piercing the fabric or stitches. Ensure the thread lies flat and covers the canvas. Insert the needle at W, under a cluster of spokes, to finish. Four straight stitches in a cross can be stitched over the joins between spokes if canvas is visible, as shown on the left.

Pinwheel Stitch

Pinwheel stitch is dynamic and decorative and works best in large areas. The spaces between pinwheels need to be filled with another stitch, which can be selected to complement other areas of the design.

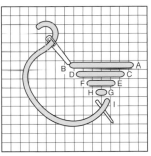

1 Make the right-hand group of stitches first, bringing the needle out at A and inserting it it B, seven strands to the left. Work C–D, E–F and G–H to complete the group. Bring the needle out at I, immediately below G, and insert it at B to start the next group.

Work I–B, J–K, L–M and N–O to form the next group. Bring the needle out at P, seven strands below B to start the next group. Work the remaining groups in the same way, moving clockwise around the central point of B.

3 The spaces between the pinwheels can be filled with either tent stitch (see page 140) as seen to the right, or diagonal stitches, which can be arranged to emphasise the squares that the pinwheels sit in, as shown.

Rhodes Stitch

Rhodes stitch makes small criss-crossed squares that can be worked in different sizes. These squares can also be worked in conjunction with cushion stitch and crossed cushion stitch (see page 144). Stitches may be worked anti-clockwise, as here, or clockwise.

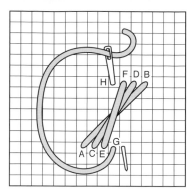

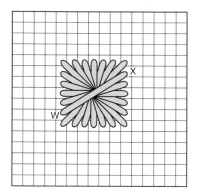

1 Bring the needle out at A on the lower right corner of the square and insert it six canvas strands above and to the right at B. Bring it out at C and insert it at D, out at E and insert it at F, and so on around the square.

2 The last stitch in the square will be W to X, as shown.

Rice Stitch

Rice stitch is good for filling small and medium areas. It can be worked in two colours or in one colour, as in a pennant in the Bunting Clutch Purse (see page 154).

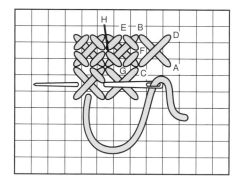

1 Working across the design area from right to left, work all the underlying crosses over two-by-two canvas strands, bringing the needle out at A and inserting it at B, out at C and inserting it at D. Then work back across the rows stitching bars across the arms of the crosses (the upper-right underlying cross is left visible here for clarity). Work E–F, G–F, H–G and E–H.

Scotch Stitch

Scotch stitch produces a simple grid texture that can be exploited in different ways. Some squares can be stitched in a contrast colour to create a motif or a geometric pattern, squares can be stitched in random colours, or in tones of a single colour to produce shading.

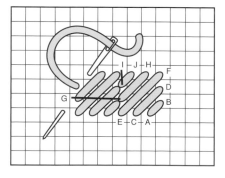

1 Starting at the top right of the design area, bring the needle out at A and insert it at B, then work C–D, E–F, G–H and I–J to complete the five stitches of the first square. Work the next square to the left, as shown.

2 To work the next row, turn the canvas and work from right to left again.

Star Stitch

Star stitch produces a very textural background that is useful for filling small and medium areas. It can be used in large areas, but is quite time-consuming and can look very busy.

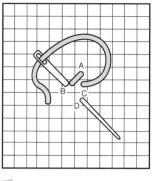

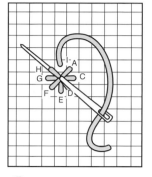

1 Bring the needle out at A at the top right of the design area. Insert it at B, which will be the centre of the stitch. Bring it out at C, insert it at B, bring it out at D and so on around the square.

2 Complete the square, stitching clockwise in turn from E, F, G, H and I to B. Bring the needle out at H to start the next stitch to the left.

3 Work the next row from right to left, working the stitches anti-clockwise and fitting the squares immediately below one another, as shown.

Turkey Stitch

Turkey stitch produces a dense, pile surface and the loops can either be left as they are, or they can be cut to produce a rug texture. This stitch is sometimes called Rya stitch.

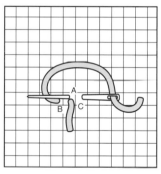

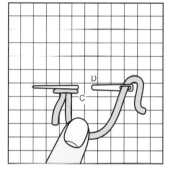

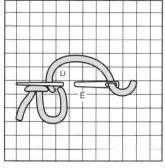

1 Starting on the bottom left of the design area, insert the needle at A and bring it out one canvas strand to the left at B, leaving a short tail of thread on the front. Insert the needle two strands to the right at C and bring it out at again A, making sure the thread is looped above the stitch, as shown.

2 Pull the thread through and pull the stitch tight. Hold down the thread with your finger and make a stitch under one strand from D to C to form the first loop.

3 Make a stitch under one strand from E to D to secure the loop. Pull this stitch tight. Work along the row to the right in this way. Cut the thread at the end of the row, leaving a short tail.

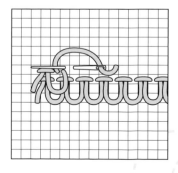

4 Start the next row on the left again, one strand above the previous row.

Bunting clutch purse

A whimsical but sophisticated little clutch purse worked in a vintage-inspired colour palette. An alternative palette of a cream background and bright pennants would give a very different feel to the same design. The making up is done entirely by hand, and is simpler than you might think.

MATERIALS

- Piece of 18-count canvas measuring 45 x 40cm (18 x 16in)
- Slate frame or roller frame
- Tape measure
- Clutch purse template (see page 171)
- Permanent marker pen
- Anchor Stranded Cotton: one skein of each of colours 11, 167, 240 and 275
- Size 24 tapestry needle
- Appleton Crewel Wool: 13 skeins of 855
- Scissors
- Pins
- Brown narrow ric-rac measuring 80cm (32in)
- Hand-sewing needle
- Sewing threads to match ric-rac and fabric
- Large snap fastener
- Piece of cotton fabric measuring 33 x 26cm (13 x 10¼in)
- Iron
- Pressing cloth
- Curved needle (optional)
- Topstitching thread to match background yarn

STITCHES USED

- Byzantine stitch (see page 142)
- Cashmere stitch (see page 142)
- Circular eyelet (see page 145)
- Cushion stitch (see page 144)
- Encroaching slanted Gobelin stitch (see page 148)
- Hungarian diamond stitch (see page 148)
- Jacquard stitch (see page 149)
- Milanese stitch (see page 150)
- Parisian stitch (see page 150)
- Rice stitch (see page 152)
- Tent stitch (see page 140)

THE EMBROIDERY

Fix the canvas into a slate frame or roller frame (see pages 18 and 19). Enlarge the template by 200 per cent and measure then tack the outline centrally onto the canvas (see page 20). Using the permanent marker pen, draw the outlines of the pennants onto the canvas (see page 15).

Use six strands of Anchor Stranded Cotton (the full thickness of the thread as it comes in the skein) unless otherwise stated. Untwist and separate the strands of each cut length, then lay them smoothly together to thread through the needle; this does make the stitches lie more neatly. Start by embroidering the pennants. With the curved flap facing you and working from right to left, embroider the first pennant on the flap with rice stitch in colour 167, using three strands for the small stitches across the arms of the cross stitches. Embroider the second pennant in Milanese stitch in colour 11 and the third pennant in Hungarian diamond using eight strands of colour 240. The fourth pennant is Milanese stitch in colour 275 and the fifth pennant is embroidered as for the first one. Start at the top centre of each pennant and work out to each side and down the length, working short stitches or tent stitches to fill the edges of the shapes, keeping them as triangular as possible.

Keeping the work facing the same way around, embroider the pennants across the back of the purse. The first one on the left is Jacquard stitch in colour 275, the next encroaching slanted Gobelin stitch in colour 240, the third cashmere stitch in colour 11, then Parisian stitch in colour 167, cushion stitch in colour 275, Byzantine stitch in colour 240 and finally circular eyelets in four strands of colour 11.

The row of the pennants across the front of the purse is the same as the previous row, but in reverse order; so the first pennant is circular eyelets in four strands of colour 11 and the last is Jacquard stitch in colour 275.

Stitch the background in cushion stitch using two strands of Appleton Crewel Wool in colour 855. Using the photograph as a guide, vary the sizes of the squares and rectangles and fill in any tiny gaps with tent stitch.

MAKING UP

Take the canvas out of the frame and cut it out 1cm (⅜in) outside the edges of the stitching.

Using the photograph as a guide, pin a length of ric-rac across the top of each row of pennants. For the row on the flap, tuck the ends of the ric-rac under to neaten them. On the other rows, leave a 1cm (⅜in) tail of ric-rac extending over the edge of the stitching on each side. Sew the ric-rac in place with matching thread, removing the pins as you go.

Fold over a hem around the curved edge of the flap, folding over the bare canvas and about 3mm (⅛in) of the stitching. Using sewing thread, backstitch the hem to the back of the cushion stitch embroidery, cutting small notches in the edge of the hem as you stitch so that it lies flat. Work oversewing stitches over the raw edge of the hem to hold it flat against the back of the embroidery. Fold over the short straight end (the front top edge of the purse) by the same amount and sew the hem in the same way.

Fold in the long side edges exactly along the edge of the stitching. Carefully snip the bulk of the bare canvas out of the corners so that they lie as flat as possible. Oversew the edges of the hems to the back of the stitching. Fold the tails of ric-rac to the back and sew them down.

Sew the socket side of the snap fastener to the right side of the front part of the purse. Position it above the line of ric-rac so that when the flap is folded over the snap is central and completely covered.

Cut the fabric lining to 1cm (⅜in) larger all around than the embroidery, then cut off 5mm (¼in) along the straight short end. Press under a 12mm (½in) hem all around. Mitre the corners and trim off as much bulk as possible. Pin the lining to the back of the embroidery so that the edges just overlap the stitching on the curved and short sides, and are one canvas strand short of the stitching on the long sides: the fabric should be very taut. Starting on one side of the flap, slip stitch the lining to the embroidery, making sure you stitch through the canvas rather than just through the woollen embroidery stitches, but being careful not to let your stitches show on the right side on the embroidery. When you have stitched the lining in place, press it through a damp cloth.

Temporarily fold the purse up (the folds are shown by dotted lines on the template) to locate where the ball side of the snap fastener should be positioned on the inside of the flap – so that it aligns with the socket sewn to the front of the purse. Sew the snap to the lining.

Fold up the purse and close the fastener. Thread a needle with topstitching thread and secure it in the fold at the bottom of one side. Sew up the side of the purse, oversewing through only the bare strand of canvas at the edge of the stitching. Thread a size 24 tapestry needle with Appleton Crewel Wool and double it. Starting from the bottom, sew straight stitches over the oversewing to cover it. Repeat on the other side of the purse.

getting it right

It's a good idea to choose a lining fabric that tones with the background wool colour, so that if when the purse is finished the fabric does show a little at the top corners, it isn't noticeable.

DRAWN THREAD

Drawn thread is a counted thread embroidery technique that is traditionally used on best-quality table linen. While it isn't a difficult technique to master, it does require careful counting and delicate handling and stitching, so it can be time-consuming. The nature of the technique means that patterns are made up of blocks and bands, but this doesn't have to mean a regimented or dull result. And although it is a traditional form of whitework, drawn thread is gorgeous worked in toning colours to emphasise its delicate nature. The Skinny Scarf (see page 164) is an ideal introduction to drawn thread; it is a sampler that you can wear. The Laundry Bag (see page 168) can be as complex or simple as you want and is both pretty and practical.

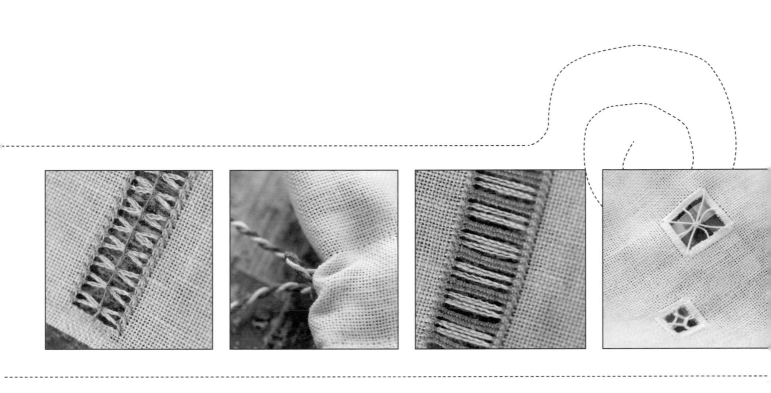

Stitching Drawn Thread

Drawn thread is a counted thread embroidery technique that, as the name suggests, involves withdrawing strands of fabric from a specific area. The remaining strands are then embroidered into different patterns. For general instructions for preparing fabric, transferring a design and starting and finishing stitching, turn to pages 14–22.

Fabrics

This technique requires an evenweave fabric (see page 8 for more details) that is not too tightly woven or it will be difficult to withdraw the threads. Try fraying a few strands from the cut edge of a piece of fabric to see how easy it will be to withdraw sections. Linen is always a good choice and a fabric of around 26 strands to the inch will usually work well. You can work single borders on any woven fabric, but be aware that corners will not be square if the fabric is not evenweave.

Threads

As table linen needs to be washed, drawn thread is traditionally worked with a sewing thread of the same fibre as the fabric, so linen thread for linen fabric. However, cotton thread is usually suitable for either linen or cotton fabrics. In the same way as pulled thread embroidery (see page 120), the sewing thread should ideally be the same thickness as the fabric strands. The best way of checking this is to pull off a strand from the edge of the fabric and lay it next to the proposed sewing thread; they should be roughly the same thickness.

   The projects in this chapter are worked in two strands of Anchor Stranded Cotton (see page 10 for more details). Other appropriate threads for this technique are Anchor Pearl Cotton no. 12 and Anchor Coton à Broder in ticket no. 16; both are suitably fine and are available in a range of colours.

Needle

Use a tapestry needle so that you push between the fabric threads rather than piercing them. A size 24 or 26 tapestry needle will usually be suitable.

Charts

Drawn thread is, like all counted thread work, stitched from a chart. The grid lines of the charts represent the strands of the fabric. The stitches need to be worked firmly enough to gather the vertical threads as illustrated on the charts, but not so tightly as to distort other strands in the fabric.

Withdrawing fabric strands

Woven fabrics have a warp thread and a weft thread and for drawn thread either or both of these can be withdrawn (see opposite) in a project. For ease of explanation, in this chapter the threads being withdrawn are referred to as the horizontal threads, and those left in place are referred to as the vertical threads. Patterns must be worked over different numbers of strands to be effective and each pattern here tells you how many strands it requires.

Starting to stitch

To work a buttonhole or satin stitch edge (see opposite), either use the in-line method (see page 22) or use a waste knot (see page 22) and darn the end into the back of the stitches later. Subsequent threads can be started by darning them into the back of the satin or buttonhole stitch, though don't darn in so many ends that the stitches become distorted. If there is no buttonhole or satin stitch to start the thread in, there are a couple of options. If you are using a thread that matches the fabric, a couple of tiny securing backstitches can be made through strands on the back of the fabric to start the thread (see page 23). Alternatively, use a waste knot placed a distance away (to create a long tail of thread) and carefully darn it into the back of the hem stitching when the work is complete. Finish stitching by darning the end into the back of adjacent stitches.

Withdrawing Strands

Withdrawing strands of the fabric is the process of cutting strands and darning in the ends to create the single strand areas that will be embroidered. This needs to be done properly for the finished work to be neat and secure. You will need a pair of small, sharp scissors for this task.

1 Work out how many vertical strands of fabric you will need to embroider the chosen stitch pattern. Using a contrast colour thread for clarity (red is used here), tack around the area where the threads are going to be withdrawn. Mark the centre of the area with a pin. Carefully cut the horizontal strands of the fabric at the marked point. You may need to use the tip of a tapestry needle to separate the strands a little before cutting them. Use the tapestry needle to unweave the strands back towards the tacking lines, making sure that the correct number of vertical strands are exposed. Thread each strand into the eye of the finest needle possible and weave them back into the fabric a short distance, as shown. Cut off loose ends as close as possible to the fabric.

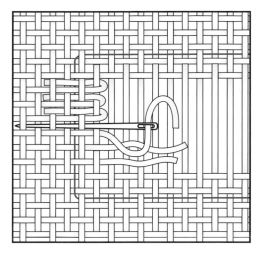

Satin Stitch

Satin stitch (see page 135) can be used to secure the vertical threads before horizontal threads are cut away. This is quicker than weaving in ends (see above), but the stitching can be obtrusive.

1 Work satin stitches over three or four vertical fabric strands at the end of the section to be cut away, as shown. Use small, sharp scissors with fine points to cut carefully though each strand of fabric next to the end of the satin stitches. Cut right up to the end of the stitches without damaging them. Then carefully withdraw the cut threads using tweezers. Threads are only cut across the end of satin stitches, not along their length.

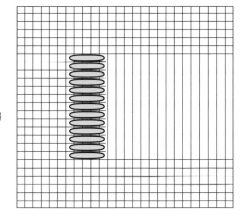

Buttonhole Stitch

Buttonhole stitch (see page 63) can be used in the same way as satin stitch (see above) to secure some threads before cutting away other ones.

1 Work buttonhole stitch over three fabric strands at the end of the section to be cut away. Cut the threads as for satin stitch.

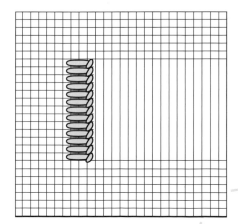

Hem Stitch

Hem stitch, in one of the various patterns shown, is a fundamental element in drawn thread embroidery. It can be worked over three to six strands of fabric per bundle. This stitch is used in both the Laundry Bag (see page 168) and the Skinny Scarf (see page 164).

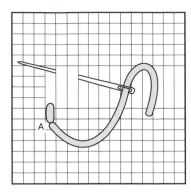

1 Bring the needle out at A, two fabric strands below the lower left-hand side of the withdrawn threads. Make a small stitch over the edge of the section, bringing the needle out at A again, as shown. From right to left, take the needle behind three (or the desired number) of vertical strands.

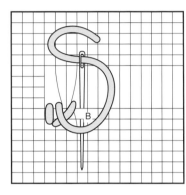

2 Pull the thread gently taut to gather the bundle of strands together. From the back, take the needle under two strands of the fabric on the lower edge of the withdrawn section, bringing it out at B. Make sure the thread lies over the needle, as shown.

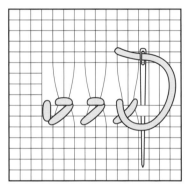

3 Take the needle behind the next bundle of three strands and repeat the stitch to the end of the withdrawn section.

Ladder Hem Stitch

Ladder hem stitch is the most commonly used hem stitch pattern. As with hem stitch (see above), it can be worked over three to six strands of fabric.

1 Work hem stitch along one edge of the withdrawn section. Turn the work and repeat the process on the other edge of the section, making sure that the same bundle of fabric strands is stitched on both edges.

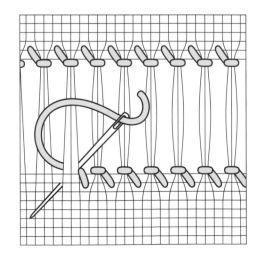

Zigzag Hem Stitch

Zigzag hem stitch is a hem stitch pattern that needs to be worked over bundles of an even number of fabric strands. Here it is shown worked over six strands. This pattern is used in the Skinny Scarf (see page 164).

1 Work hem stitch along one edge of the withdrawn section. Turn the work and hem stitch the other edge, but split each bundle of strands in half, stitching each half together with half of the adjacent bundle, as shown. At the beginning and end you will need to make bundles of just half the number of strands.

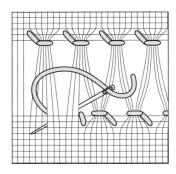

Double Hem Stitch

Double hem stitch can be worked over three to six fabric strands. To form this stitch pattern two areas of strands need to be withdrawn, leaving a section with four to six horizontal strands of fabric between them. This pattern is also used in the Skinny Scarf (see page 164).

1 Starting on the top right-hand side of the lower withdrawn section, take the needle from A to B right around the first bundle of fabric strands. On the back of the work, make a diagonal stitch, bringing the needle out at C. Encircle the same bundle of strands, bringing the needle back to C. On the front of the work, make a diagonal stitch down to D. Repeat to the end of the section.

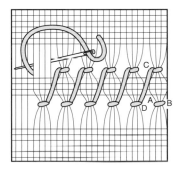

Interlaced Hem Stitch

Interlaced hem stitch is a decorative variation of hem stitch. The interlacing can be done with thread, as here and in the Skinny Scarf (see page 164), or with ribbon, as in the Laundry Bag (see page 168). The withdrawn section needs to be wide enough to accommodate the interlacing material, plus space on either side, and there must be an even number of bundles.

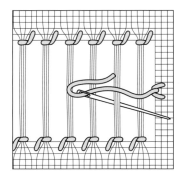

1 Ladder hem stitch (see opposite, below) the withdrawn section, with three to six fabric strands in each bundle. Secure the interlacing thread to the centre of the right-hand end of the section. Take the needle from left to right under the second bundle of threads and over the first bundle.

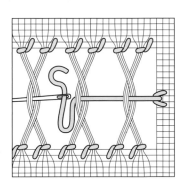

2 Twist the needle to face in the opposite direction and pull the thread through. Repeat with each subsequent pair of bundles.

Knotted Border Stitch

Knotted border stitch offers another way of embellishing a ladder-stitched hem. The bundles can be of three to six fabric strands and the number of bundles must be divisible by three. This stitch is also used in the Skinny Scarf (see page 164).

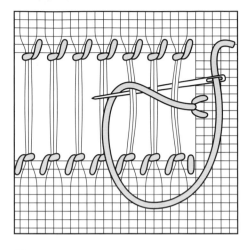

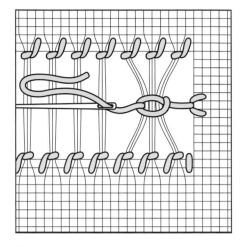

1 Ladder hem stitch (see page 160) the withdrawn section. Secure the lacing thread to the centre of the right-hand end of the section. Loop the thread over the first three bundles, as shown, and take the needle under them and through the thread loop.

2 Pull the loop taut to gather the three bundles together. Repeat across the withdrawn section.

Overcast Bars

Overcast bars consist of strands of fabric wrapped with thread to make chunky bundles. The bundles can be of three to six strands and the number of strands in the withdrawn area must be divisible by the number required for each bundle.

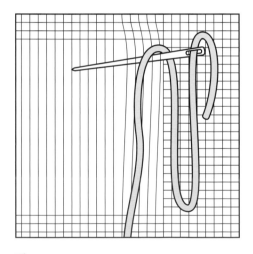

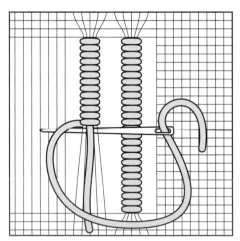

1 Lay the tail end of the thread along the fabric strands of the first bundle and take the needle under the thread and the strands, as shown.

2 Wrap the thread around the bundle and keep wrapping to overcast the strands. After the first three wraps, gently pull the tail taut and use the tip of the needle to slide the wraps right to the top of the bundle. As you wrap, continue to ease the loops of thread up to sit tightly together. At the bottom of the bar, carefully slide the needle up the back of a few wraps, pull taut and cut off the thread as close to the bar as possible. Trim the initial tail as well.

Zigzag Overcast Bars

Zigzag overcast bars are a variation of overcast bars (see opposite, below) and the number of vertical fabric strands in the withdrawn section must be divisible by the number required for each bundle. These bars feature in the Skinny Scarf (see page 164).

1 Overcast the first bar on the right of the withdrawn section, but do not finish off the thread at the bottom. Instead, for the last wrap, take the thread around the strands of the working bundle and the adjacent bundle. Then continue wrapping up the strands of the adjacent bundle, as shown. At the top, wrap the bundle to the next one and wrap down that bundle. Repeat to overcast all the bars.

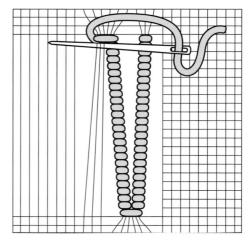

Woven Bars

Woven bars must be formed from an even number of strands; here six are used. The tail of the thread is caught into the bar in the same way as for overcast bars (see opposite), and the bars can be worked top to bottom or vice versa. Woven bars are used in the Skinny Scarf (see page 164).

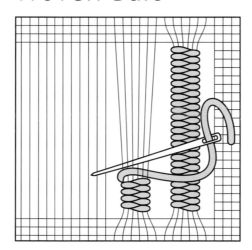

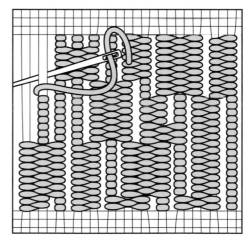

1 Take the needle over the three left-hand strands, then under the three right-hand strands. Take it over the three right-hand strands and under the three left-hand ones, as shown. Weave up the bar in this way, sliding the wraps close together with the tip of the needle. Finish the thread as for overcast bars.

2 With a bit of planning, strands and bundles can be woven to form decorative bar patterns in a withdrawn area. Pairs of strands can be overcast while larger bundles are woven. You may need to start or finish bundles midway to create the patterns you require.

Skinny scarf

A perfect accessory for a summer wedding or lunch party, this simple scarf makes best use of a variety of easy-to-work stitch patterns. If you make your own clothes, then make the scarf from the same fabric as part of your outfit for a very coordinated look.

MATERIALS

- Piece of 28-count evenweave fabric in blue/grey measuring 20cm (8in) by as long as required
- Tacking thread
- Hand-sewing needle
- 20cm (8in) ring frame
- Tape measure
- Anchor Stranded Cotton: one skein of each of colours 161, 167, and 168
- Size 26 tapestry needle
- Scissors
- Iron
- Pins
- Sewing thread to match fabric

STITCHES USED

- Double hem stitch (see page 161)
- Hem stitch (see page 160)
- Interlaced hem stitch (see page 161)
- Knotted border stitch (see page 162)
- Ladder hem stitch (see page 160)
- Withdrawing strands (see page 159)
- Woven bars (see page 163)
- Zigzag hem stitch (see page 161)
- Zigzag overcast bars (see page 163)

THE EMBROIDERY

Tacking along the weave of the fabric, tack two lines spaced 8cm (3in) apart along the strip of fabric, positioning them centrally. Put one end of the fabric at a time into a large ring frame (see page 18) – it won't fill the frame in both directions, but that won't matter as long as you tighten the frame as much as possible. At each end of the scarf, each of the three bands of embroidery consists of 16 horizontal strands of fabric withdrawn across 84 vertical strands, and the ends are woven in for 1.5cm (⅝in) beyond the tacking stitches. The first band at each end is 7cm (2¾in) up from the edge and the subsequent bands are 4cm (1½in) apart (you can count the number of strands in one 4cm (1½in) measurement and space the bars the same number of strands apart if you prefer). All the stitching is done using two strands of Stranded Cotton.

At one end, use colour 161 to ladder hem stitch the withdrawn band with three strands in each bundle. Then work knotted border stitch across the band. The next band up uses colour 168 to work zigzag overcast bars with four strands in each bar. The third band uses colour 167 to work zigzag hem stitch with two strands in each bundle.

At the other end of the fabric, the first band uses colour 161 to work double hem stitch with three strands in each bundle. The next band uses colour 168 to work hem stitch with two strands in each bundle. These strands are then woven into bars with two bundles (four strands) in each bar. The third band uses colour 167 to work interlaced hem stitch with three strands in each bundle.

MAKING UP

To prevent the fabric fraying while you work, it is best to cut and hem the scarf a short section at a time. Cut the fabric to 1.5cm (⅝in) outside one tacking line. Turn over and pin a double 5mm (¼in) hem, so the inner folded edge is on the tacking line. Using matching thread, slip stitch the hem in place, removing the tacking stitches as you go. Repeat on the other side of the scarf. I have used the selvedge edges of the fabric as the lower edges of the scarf (I carefully picked out the strand of contrast colour) but you could turn under and hem the short ends in the same way as the sides; mitring the corners would reduce bulk.

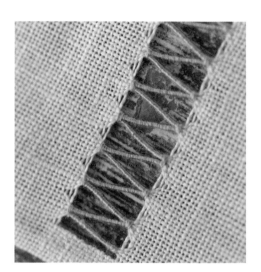

getting it right

As you are only withdrawing bands in one direction, the fabric used for the scarf doesn't have to be evenweave, though it does need to be woven. If you wanted to simplify the stitching, you could work just one band at each end, or several bands of the same stitch.

Buttonhole Corner

Buttonhole corners are the basis for a number of filled corner patterns. The corner is created when both the warp and weft threads are withdrawn from an area, leaving it completely open.

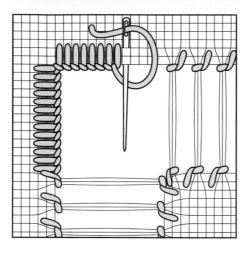

1 Withdraw the threads and hem stitch the borders as required (see pages 159 and 160). Using buttonhole stitch (see page 63), and working into every hole in the fabric, stitch around the free edges of the hole. You can also use buttonhole stitch to secure the ends of a border and then cut away the threads (see page 159).

Ribbed Square Corner

Ribbed square corner is the simplest of the filled corners to construct and it features in the Laundry Bag (see page 168). Start by working a buttonhole corner (see above).

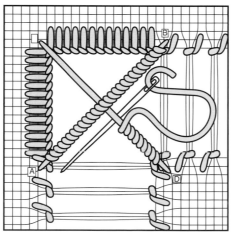

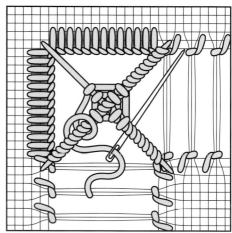

1 Secure the thread on the back of the buttonhole stitches and bring it out at A. Make a diagonal stitch to insert the needle at B and bring it out through the open corner at the same point. Do not pull the stitch too tight or the square corner will be distorted. Overcast the stitch as for an overcast bar (see page 162) back to A. Run the needle through the back of the buttonhole stitches to C and insert it at D. Bring it through and overcast it to where the two stitches cross in the middle.

2 Starting from the centre of the cross, take the needle over a spoke then under it and under the adjacent spoke. Repeat around the spokes to work a square version of a ribbed wheel (see page 60). Finish the ribbing on the strand not yet overcast, then overcast it to complete the corner.

Wheel Corner

Wheel corners are a more elaborate version of ribbed square corners (see opposite, below) and can only be worked when the borders either side of the corner have been interlaced (see page 161). The interlacing threads form a square cross across the open corner. Wheel corners feature in the Laundry Bag (see page 168).

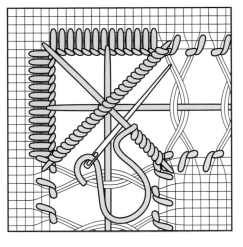

1 Work a diagonal thread cross and overcast it in the same way as for a ribbed square corner.

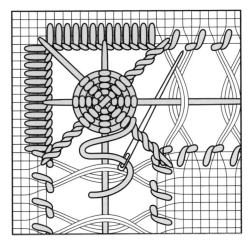

2 Starting from the centre, work as for the ribbed square corner to work a full ribbed wheel (see page 60) around the eight spokes. Finish by overcasting the remaining diagonal strand.

Woven Corner

Woven corners are a variation of wheel corners (see above). Prepare the corner and diaonal cross as for a wheel corner.

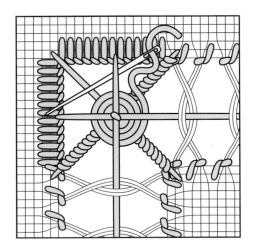

1 Work one wrapping stitch over the centre of the spokes to hold them all together. Starting from the centre, take the needle under square spokes and over diagonal spokes to weave a wheel. As there are an even number of spokes, be careful not to pull the thread up tightly and so distort the round shape. Finish by overcasting the remaining diagonal strand.

Laundry bag

Proving that drawn thread work can look both contemporary and pretty, the embroidery on this stylish laundry bag can be as complex as you want it to be: work just the band and a couple of the simplest squares, or scatter a variety.

MATERIALS

- Piece of 28-count evenweave fabric in white measuring 60 x 45cm (24 x18in)
- Tape measure
- Tacking thread
- Hand-sewing needle
- Roller frame
- Small, sharp scissors
- Anchor Stranded Cotton: two skeins of colour 1
- Size 26 tapestry needle
- Piece of 1-cm (⅜-in) wide white cotton ribbon measuring 50cm (20in) long
- Scissors
- Two pieces of cotton fabric and one piece of 28-count evenweave fabric in white measuring 50 x 33cm (20 x 13in)
- White sewing thread
- Sewing machine
- Two 90cm (35in) pieces of cord, made or bought

STITCHES USED

- Buttonhole corner (see page 166)
- Buttonhole stitch (see page 159)
- Dove's eye filling stitch (see page 55)
- Interlaced hem stitch (see page 161)
- Overcast bars (see page 162)
- Ribbed square corner (see page 166)
- Wheel corner (see page 167)
- Withdrawing strands (see page 159)
- Woven corner (see page 167)

THE EMBROIDERY

Tacking along the weave of the fabric, tack a 50 x 33cm (20 x 13in) rectangle onto the larger piece of evenweave fabric, positioning it centrally; this is the size of the bag. Tack a horizontal line 13cm (5in) down from one short edge; the 37 x 33cm (15 x 13in) space below this line will be where the embroidery is worked. Fix the area to be embroidered into a roller frame (see page 18). All stitching is worked with two strands of Stranded Cotton unless otherwise stated.

Starting 10cm (4in) up from the bottom edge, withdraw a 2-cm (¾-in) wide band of horizontal strands across 330 vertical strands: position the withdrawn band centrally so that there is a seam allowance of about 1cm (⅜in) of fabric within the tacked rectangle. Work hem stitch with three strands in each bundle on both sides of the withdrawn band. Interlace the stitches with the piece of white ribbon, leaving the ends of the ribbon extending beyond the tacked rectangle.

Position the squares randomly on the fabric. Each one is made by working a square of buttonhole stitch over 12 to 22 strands, then cutting the strands in both directions: the principle is the same as for creating a buttonhole corner, but without the withdrawn bands on either side. Fill the open squares with whichever stitches you prefer. Here, the squares with a simple star in them are made by constructing the interlacing threads as for a wheel corner, but just overcasting them rather

than adding the ribbed circle. The squares with the diamond-shaped, looped stitches in them have borrowed the dove's eye filling stitch from the Hardanger chapter, and use three strands of thread. The other corner fillings are all traditional to drawn thread work.

MAKING UP

Take the embroidered fabric out of the frame and cut it down to the outer tacking lines, then remove the tacking stitches. Lay one piece of backing fabric flat face-up and lay the embroidered fabric face-up on top of it, matching all edges. Pin the pieces together. Set the sewing machine to a narrow zigzag stitch and sew the layers together all around the edges. Repeat the process with the other piece of backing fabric and evenweave fabric.

Lay the two pieces evenweave-sides together, matching all edges, and pin. Set the sewing machine to a small straight stitch and, taking a 1cm (⅜in) seam allowance, stitch down one long side for 11cm (4½in) from the top short edge. Reverse to secure the stitching and cut the threads. Leave a gap of 1.5cm (⅝in), then sew the rest of the side seam. Repeat on the other long side, then sew the bottom seam.

Set the machine to a narrow zigzag stitch and sew around the seam allowances, as close as possible to the stitching and keeping the pattern of gaps in the side seams. Trim the seam allowances close to the zigzagging. Turn the bag right side out and press it.

At the top edge, turn over 7cm (2¾in) to the wrong side and press. Sew the hem, stitching 5mm (¼in) from the zigzagged edge. Sew a second line, 2.5cm (1in) up from the first, to create a channel; the openings in the side seams should be within this channel.

If you want to make cord, see the Bargello Cushion instructions (see page 146). Thread a length of cord through one opening, around the channel and out through the same opening, and knot the ends. Repeat with the second cord, but using the opposite opening. Pull both cords to close the bag.

Templates and Charts

All templates are shown at 50%, except
for Acorns and Oak Leaves and Silver
Brooch, which are shown at 100%.

Sleeping Mask, page 94

Celebration Bunting,
page 34

Retro Sunglasses
Case, page 42

Acorns and Oak
Leaves, page 116

Bird Book Bag, page 82

Silver Brooch,
page 112

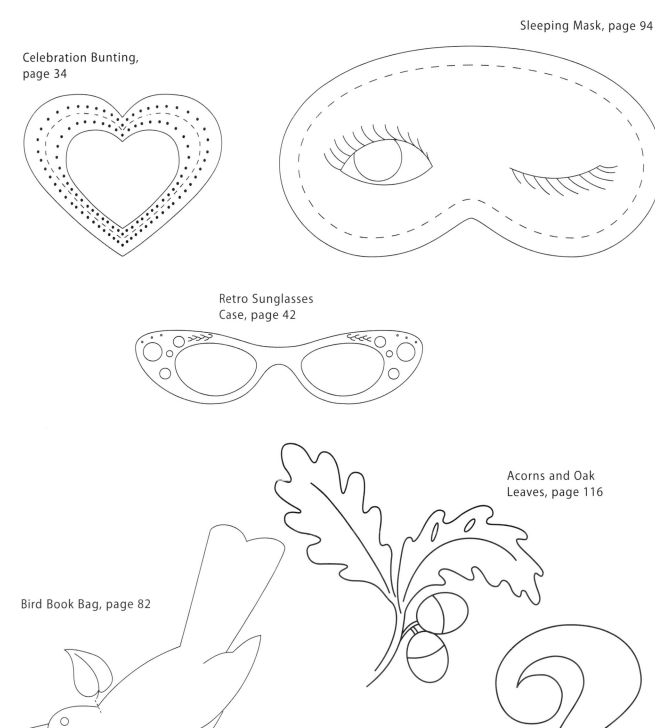

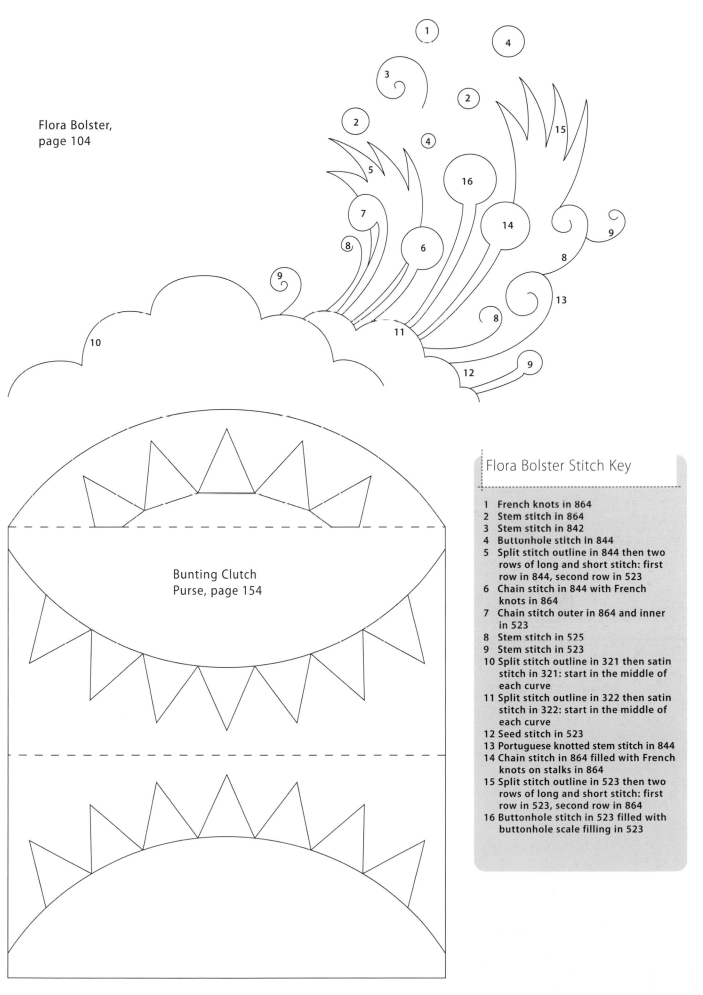

Flora Bolster,
page 104

Bunting Clutch
Purse, page 154

Flora Bolster Stitch Key

1 French knots in 864
2 Stem stitch in 864
3 Stem stitch in 842
4 Buttonhole stitch in 844
5 Split stitch outline in 844 then two
   rows of long and short stitch: first
   row in 844, second row in 523
6 Chain stitch in 844 with French
   knots in 864
7 Chain stitch outer in 864 and inner
   in 523
8 Stem stitch in 525
9 Stem stitch in 523
10 Split stitch outline in 321 then satin
   stitch in 321: start in the middle of
   each curve
11 Split stitch outline in 322 then satin
   stitch in 322: start in the middle of
   each curve
12 Seed stitch in 523
13 Portuguese knotted stem stitch in 844
14 Chain stitch in 864 filled with French
   knots on stalks in 864
15 Split stitch outline in 523 then two
   rows of long and short stitch: first
   row in 523, second row in 864
16 Buttonhole stitch in 523 filled with
   buttonhole scale filling in 523

Snowflake Drawstring Bag, page 24

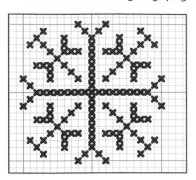

Smartphone Case, page 56

Diamond Bracelet, page 128

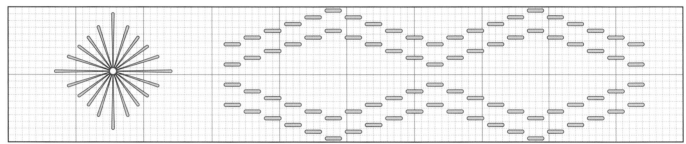

Clouds Peg Bag, page 64

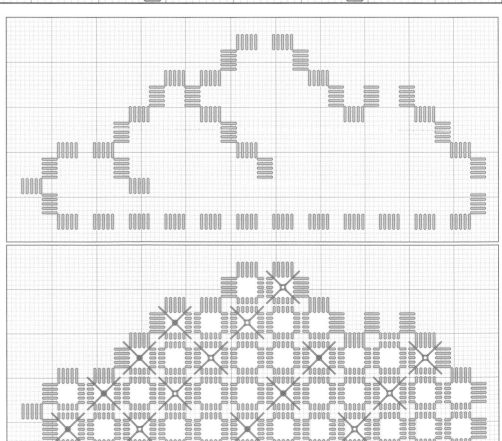

Spider's web filling stitch

Oblique loop filling stitch

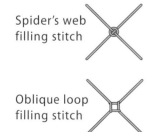

Cupcake Apron,
page 136

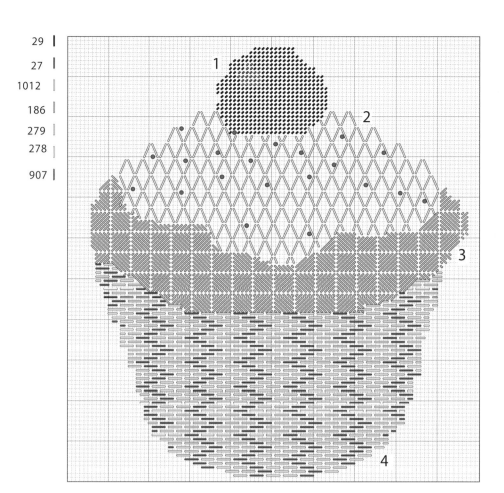

29
27
1012
186
279
278
907

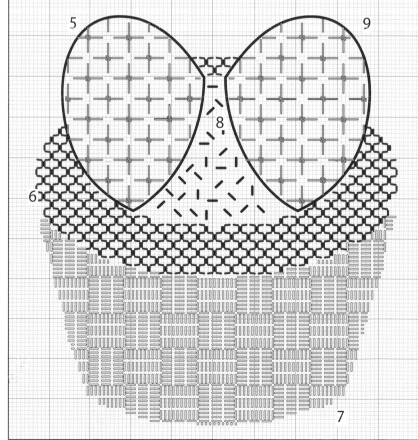

11
40
240
278/
279

Cupcake Apron Stitch Key

1 Tent stitch
2 Wave stitch
3 Diagonal satin filling
4 Florentine stitch
5 Stem stitch
6 Honeycomb filling
7 Chessboard filling (alternate blocks of 278/279)
8 Straight stitches (2 strands)
9 Greek cross stitch lacy filling (2 strands)

Suppliers

Appleton Brothers
Thames Works
Church Street
Chiswick
London W4 2PE
Tel: 020 8994 0711
Web: www.embroiderywool.co.uk
(Crewel and tapestry wools)

Coats Crafts UK
Green Lane Mill
Holmfirth
HD9 2DX
Tel: 00 44 (0) 1484 681 881
Email: consumer.ccuk@coats.com
Web: www.coatscrafts.co.uk
(Embroidery threads)

Fabrics Galore
54 Lavender Hill
London SW11 5RH
Tel: 020 7738 9589
Email: fabricsgalore@btinternet.com
Web: www.fabricsgalore.com
(Excellent selection of fabrics, and at
great prices)

Golden Threads
Brimstone Cottage
Pounsley
Blackboys
East Sussex TN22 5HS
Email: info@goldenthreads.co.uk
Web: www.goldenthreads.co.uk
(Metal threads)

Royal School of Needlework
Apartment 12a
Hampton Court Palace
Surrey KT8 9AU
Tel: 020 3166 6932
Email: enquiries@royal-needlework.org.uk
Web: www.royal-needlework.org.uk
(Embroidery courses, equipment and
materials)

Bargello Cushion,
page 146

9790
8018
8596
8592
8590
8586

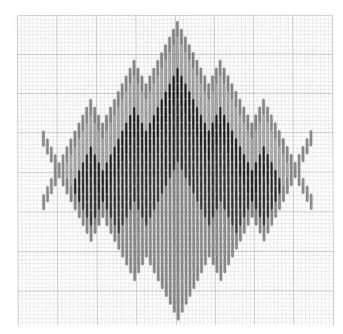

Acknowledgments

I would like to thank Katy Denny for commissioning this book and
for being generally marvellous. A huge thank you to Becky for her
beautiful stitching and constantly good-humoured help. My thanks
also to Cheryl for her editorial expertise, Jeni and Sarah at D&C for
their editorial and design work, Steve for his consistently excellent
illustrations, and to Sian for taking the gorgeous photographs. My
heartfelt thanks, as ever, to Philip for the food.

About the Author

Kate Haxell is an author and editor who has written and worked
on numerous best-selling craft and design books. A grandma who
taught her to sew and knit at an early age, a degree in art and
design, a job as a magazine stylist all contributed to allowing Kate to
make a living doing things she loves – and she feels very lucky. Visit
Kate's website at www.katehaxell.co.uk.

Becky Hogg is an embroiderer based in London. She trained in
textiles at Loughborough College of Art and in hand embroidery at
the Royal School of Needlework. Now she divides her time between
teaching, client commissions and producing a range of embroidery
kits. Visit Becky's website and shop at www.beckyhogg.com or
contact her at becky@beckyhogg.com.

Index

A DAVID & CHARLES BOOK
© F&W Media International, Ltd 2012

David & Charles is an imprint of F&W Media International, Ltd
Brunel House, Forde Close, Newton Abbot, TQ12 4PU, UK

F&W Media International, Ltd is a subsidiary of F+W Media, Inc
10151 Carver Road, Cincinnati OH45242, USA

Text © Kate Haxell 2012
Layout, projects and photography © F&W Media International, Ltd 2012
Original artworks reproduced by kind permission of Coats Crafts
Additional artworks by Stephen Dew and © F&W Media International, Ltd

First published in the UK and USA in 2012

The author and publisher have made every effort to ensure that all the
instructions in the book are accurate and safe, and therefore cannot accept
liability for any resulting injury, damage or loss to persons or property, however
it may arise.

Names of manufacturers and product ranges are provided for the information of
readers, with no intention to infringe copyright or trademarks.

A catalogue record for this book is available from the British Library.

ISBN-13: 978-1-4463-0166-1 Paperback
ISBN-10: 1-4463-0166-4 Paperback

Printed in China by RR Donnelley for:
F&W Media International, Ltd
Brunel House, Forde Close, Newton Abbot, TQ12 4PU, UK

10 9 8 7 6 5 4 3 2 1

Acquisitions Editor: Katy Denny
Desk Editor: Jeni Hennah
Proofreader: Cheryl Brown
Design Manager: Sarah Clark
Photographer: Sian Irvine
Senior Production Controller: Kelly Smith

F+W Media publishes high quality books on a wide range of subjects.
For more great book ideas visit: **www.rucraft.co.uk**